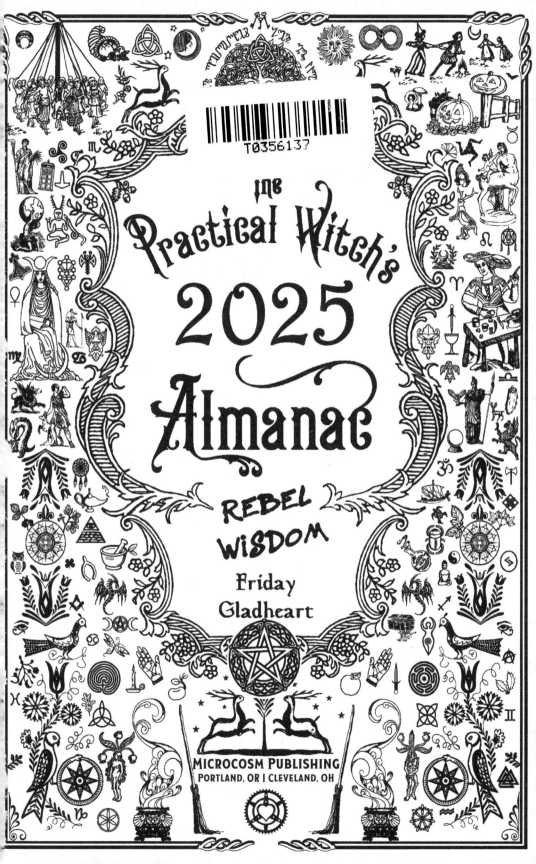

The Practical Witch's

2025

Almanac

REBEL WISDOM

Friday
Gladheart

MICROCOSM PUBLISHING
PORTLAND, OR | CLEVELAND, OH

THE PRACTICAL WITCH'S ALMANAC 2025
REBEL WISDOM
© 2024 Friday Gladheart
© This edition Microcosm Publishing 2024
First edition
ISBN 978-1648412172

To join the ranks of high-class stores that feature
Microcosm titles, talk to your rep: In the U.S. COMO
(Atlantic), ABRAHAM (Midwest), BOB BARNETT (Texas,
Oklahoma, Arkansas, Louisiana), IMPRINT (Pacific),
TURNAROUND (UK), UTP/MANDA (Canada), NEWSOUTH
(Australia/New Zealand), Observatoire (Africa, Europe), IPR
(Middle East), Yvonne Chau (Southeast Asia), HarperCollins
(India), Everest/B.K. Agency (China), Tim Burland (Japan/
Korea), and FAIRE and EMERALD in the gift trade.

For a catalog, write or visit:
Microcosm Publishing
2752 N Williams Ave.
Portland, OR 97227

All the news that's fit to print at
www.Microcosm.Pub/Newsletter

Get more copies of this book at
www.Microcosm.Pub/PWA2025

Find previous versions of The Practical Witch's Almanac at
www.Microcosm.Pub/PracticalWitch

The data in this almanac is calculated for Central
Time. It is easy to convert the data to any time zone with
the information on pages 188 and 189.

Table of Contents

How to Use Your Almanac

Lunar Planner Pages

The Lunar Planner Pages help you track the moon phases throughout the month to plan your magical and everyday activities. These pages make it easy to match the moon phase with the day of the week for nuanced magic and energy work. There's extra space next to the calendar at the top for your notes.

Weekly Planner Pages

When you reach the Weekly Planner Pages, the page borders change, making it easy to find the section you're looking for as you flip through your almanac. There is extra room for notes at the beginning of the week. You'll discover lunar data on the left side of each day's section. For example, on January 9–11, as shown here, you'll see that on Thursday, the Moon is sextile Mars at 4:49 pm, making it "void of course" (VC), and later that evening, it enters the sign of Gemini.

The term "void of course" refers to a period when the Moon isn't forming any major aspects with other planets before transitioning into a new sign. This knowledge can empower your planning. For instance, on Thursday, the Moon is VC from 4:49 pm until it enters Gemini at 7:07 pm. On Friday, the Moon goes VC again when it squares Saturn at 9:15 pm.

February Lunar Planner

February

M	T	W	T	F	S	S
					1	2
3	4	5	6	7	8	9
10	11	12	13	14	15	16
17	18	19	20	21	22	23
24	25	26	27	28		

Get seed potatoes for the garden at the farm store.

Get insurance quotes before April's renewal.

Black History Month
Library Lovers Month
Great American Pie Month

Sa	1	◑ 4:20 pm	Coven gathering 9 pm	✦
Su	2	◑	Private Sabbat celebration	
Mo	3	◑	Removing obstacles & blocks meditation	⊗

At the bottom left corner of each day's section, you'll find a rich array of notations about general holidays, events, and observances. These range from significant cultural celebrations to fun and entertaining events that spark curiosity and inspire creativity. They can also add a touch of joy to your day.

Occasionally, you'll see italicized notations below these events. These are energy notes derived from historical data, astrological information, and psychic impressions. Some of these impressions aren't specific to a day or week but apply to the entire year. This year, the themes include: More space exploration, AI will be everywhere, Chamomile (the official herb of the year), and More sightings of the Northern Lights.

January

M	T	W	T	F	S	S
		1	2	3	4	5
6	7	8	9	10	11	12
(13)	14	15	16	17	18	19
20	21	22	23	24	25	26
27	28	●29	30	31		

February

M	T	W	T	F	S	S
					□1	2
3	4	5	6	7	8	9
10	11	(12)	13	14	15	16
17	18	19	20	21	22	23
24	25	26	●27	28		

May

M	T	W	T	F	S	S
			□1	2	3	4
5	6	7	8	9	10	11
(12)	13	14	15	16	17	18
19	20	21	22	23	24	25
●26	27	28	29	30	31	

June

M	T	W	T	F	S	S
						1
2	3	4	5	6	7	8
9	10	(11)	12	13	14	15
16	17	18	19	□20	21	22
23	24	●25	26	27	28	29
30						

September

M	T	W	T	F	S	S
1	2	3	4	5	6	(7)
8	9	10	11	12	13	14
15	16	17	18	19	20	●21
□22	23	24	25	26	27	28
29	30					

October

M	T	W	T	F	S	S
	1	2	3	4	5	
(6)	7	8	9	10	11	12
13	14	15	16	17	18	19
20	●21	22	23	24	25	26
27	28	29	30	□31		

● New Moons   ○ Full Moons   □ Sabbats

March

M	T	W	T	F	S	S
					1	2
3	4	5	6	7	8	9
10	11	12	13	(14)	15	16
17	18	19	[20]	21	22	23
24	25	26	27	28	●29	30
31						

April

M	T	W	T	F	S	S
	1	2	3	4	5	6
7	8	9	10	11	(12)	13
14	15	16	17	18	19	20
21	22	23	24	25	26	●27
28	29	30				

July

M	T	W	T	F	S	S
	1	2	3	4	5	6
7	8	9	(10)	11	12	13
14	15	16	17	18	19	20
21	22	23	●24	25	26	27
28	29	30	31			

August

M	T	W	T	F	S	S
				[1]	2	3
4	5	6	7	8	(9)	10
11	12	13	14	15	16	17
18	19	20	21	22	●23	24
25	26	27	28	29	30	31

November

M	T	W	T	F	S	S
					1	2
3	4	(5)	6	7	8	9
10	11	12	13	14	15	16
17	18	19	●20	21	22	23
24	25	26	27	28	29	30

December

M	T	W	T	F	S	S
1	2	3	(4)	5	6	7
8	9	10	11	12	13	14
15	16	17	18	●19	20	[21]
22	23	24	25	26	27	28
29	30	31				

Rebel Wisdom

When you first start exploring witchcraft, it's all about learning. You dive into magic, correspondences, deities, and rituals or set personal goals to absorb as much as possible. You might follow a tradition with a structured degree system that requires extensive study. This knowledge is invaluable in developing your practice, yet it's just the beginning.

> *Knowledge is knowing what to say; wisdom is knowing whether or not to say it. Knowledge gives answers; wisdom asks questions.*
>
> ~Starhawk[1]

As you continue your journey, you transform this knowledge into wisdom through experience and practice. Wisdom also develops through critically reflecting on your practices to ensure they are still meaningful. This year's almanac encourages you to scrutinize some of the most iconic traditions of modern witchcraft—not as an attack on these foundations but as a means to gain a deeper understanding and ensure their continued relevance for you.

This process involves questioning the origins of modern witchcraft beliefs, understanding their historical and cultural contexts, and considering the evidence that supports or contradicts them. Regularly scrutinizing and reflecting on your practice helps you rebel against stagnation and complacency.

---

1   Starhawk. *The Spiral Dance*. United Kingdom: Harper & Row, 1989.

Witchcraft is an evolving practice you can refine and enhance to grow with you, leading to a more profound and authentic connection with your path. Ultimately, you decide which aspects of your practice have maintained relevance, and wisdom grows through this consideration.

Pay Attention to Your Triggers

Social Media Fatigue

Staying mindful of your triggers as you explore your beliefs and practices is crucial. One thing to watch out for is rage-bait: content designed to provoke anger and outrage. Thanks to algorithms prioritizing engagement, rage-bait is prevalent on social media— it's all about getting those clicks, shares, and comments.

Unfortunately, the cacophony of reactionary posts tends to drown out measured discourse and thoughtful discussion. After spending time online, it's easy to feel defensive or retreat into echo chambers where your viewpoints aren't challenged. While this reaction is understandable online, you must continue challenging yourself in your practice.

If the challenge of scrutinizing your practices raises triggers, try to discover the cause. Were you already on the defense from exposure to social media, or is it something else? Scrutinizing your traditions and practices does not invalidate them.

Rising Religious Extremism

There has been a noticeable increase in religious symbols in public spaces, such as courthouses, public buildings, and daily commutes. There is increasingly more religious iconography and messages on the airwaves, with radio stations adopting religious programming and an uptick in political and religiously-themed advertisements and spam in our digital lives.

Meanwhile, the rights of LGBTQIA+ people, women, and marginalized communities are under attack, and school and library meetings are bowing to outraged religious conservatives. Many people find these increasingly common religious symbols and messages intrusive, particularly in a society that values the separation of church and state.

The omnipresence of religious content can contribute to a sense of feeling cornered or pressured to conform to a particular set of beliefs. This environment can be challenging for witches and others whose spiritual practices fall outside mainstream religious traditions. When we already feel threatened, it isn't easy to scrutinize our practices.

Nevertheless, as witches, we must continually challenge ourselves to evaluate our craft to maintain its relevance. We understand that wisdom comes from a willingness to rebel against stagnation, even within our belief structures and traditions.

Embrace, Adapt, or Boldly Defy

As practical witches, our nature inclines us to rebel against anything that no longer serves a meaningful purpose. This innate rebelliousness drives us to evolve and refine our practices continuously. When you feel disconnected from your witchcraft, it is a signal to take a closer look and assess which aspects are stagnating, constricting, or outdated. This self-examination is not a sign of failure but a mark of your commitment to growth and transformation.

You have chosen to rise to the challenge of exploring your craft more deeply, demonstrating your courage and dedication. You are a witch, a "wise one," a seeker of truth and change. This journey is an opportunity to reconnect with your practice's essence and rediscover what resonates with you. As you stand at this crossroads, consider: Will you embrace the familiar, adapt to new insights, or boldly defy and redefine your established practices? Your path is your own, and this willingness to question and transform is the essence of being a witch.

Traditional Sabbat Dates

A range of approximate dates is provided because Sabbat celebrations vary by tradition and the alignment of the Earth and Sun. Equinoxes and Solstices occur at precise moments in time and may fall on different dates in different parts of the world.

Cross-Quarter Sabbats or Fire Festival are Imbolc, Beltane, Lughnasadh, and Samhain. Traditionally, these Sabbats are celebrated on the dates indicated below, but for precise astronomical times for 2025 see the Exact Sabbat Times & Dates tables on the following pages.

Approximate Dates	Northern Hemisphere	Southern Hemisphere
February 1-2	**Imbolc** Candlemas	**Lughnasadh** Lammas
March 19-21	**Ostara** Spring Equinox	**Mabon** Autumn Equinox
April 30-May 1	**Beltane** May Eve	**Samhain** Hallows
June 20-22	**Midsummer** Litha Summer Solstice	**Yule** Winter Solstice
August 1-2	**Lughnasadh** Lammas	**Imbolc** Candlemas
September 21-24	**Mabon** Autumn Equinox	**Ostara** Spring Equinox
October 31-November 1	**Samhain** Hallows	**Beltane** May Eve
December 20-23	**Yule** Winter Solstice	**Midsummer** Litha Summer Solstice

Exact Sabbat Times & Dates

2025 Northern Hemisphere

Sabbat	Eastern UTC-5	Central UTC-6	Mountain UTC-7	Pacific UTC-8
Imbolc Candlemas	**February 3**			
	9:02 am	8:02 am	7:02 am	6:02 am
Ostara Spring Equinox	**March 20**			
	5:01 am	*4:01 am*	*3:01 am*	*2:01 am*
Beltane May Eve	**May 5**		**May 4**	
	1:49 am	*12:49 am*	*11:49 pm*	*10:49 pm*
Midsummer Litha Summer Solstice	**June 20**			
	10:42 pm	*9:42 pm*	*8:42 pm*	*7:42 pm*
Lughnasadh Lammas	**August 7**		**August 6**	
	1:44 am	*12:44 am*	*11:44 pm*	*10:44 pm*
Mabon Autumn Equinox	**September 22**			
	2:19 pm	*1:19 pm*	*12:19 pm*	*11:19 am*
Samhain Hallows	**November 6**			
	10:56 pm	9:56 pm	8:56 pm	7:56 pm
Yule Winter Solstice	**December 21**			
	10:02 am	9:02 am	8:02 am	7:02 am

Time shown in *italics* is calculated for DST from Mar. 9th through Nov. 2nd.

Exact Sabbat Times & Dates

2025 Southern Hemisphere & UTC+8

Sabbat	Australia AWST UTC+8	Australia AEST UTC+10	New Zealand NZST
Lughnasadh Lammas	**Feb 3**	**February 4**	
	10:02 pm	12:02 am	2:02 am
Mabon Autumn Equinox	**March 20**		
	5:01 pm	7:01 pm	9:01 pm
Samhain Hallows	**May 5**		
	1:49 am	3:49 pm	5:49 pm
Yule Winter Solstice	**June 21**		
	10:42 pm	12:42 pm	2:42 pm
Imbolc Candlemas	**August 7**		
	1:44 am	3:44 am	5:44 am
Ostara Spring Equinox	**September 23**		
	2:19 pm	4:19 pm	6:19 am
Beltane May Eve	**November 7**		
	11:56 pm	1:56 pm	3:56 pm
Midsummer Litha Summer Solstice	**December 22**		
	11:02 am	1:02 am	3:02 am

UTC+8 includes Western Australia, China, Malaysia, Philippines, Taiwan, Hong Kong, Singapore, Brunei, and parts of Russia, Mongolia, Korea, and Indonesia.

Understanding the Sabbats

Sabbats are seasonal festivals known for their magical energy, celestial symmetry, and spiritual significance. Each Sabbat is known by various names, reflecting differences in traditions and teachings. One witch may refer to the June solstice as *Litha*, while another will call it *Midsummer*. Regardless of the names, most witches celebrate the eight classic Sabbats of four Quarters and four Cross-Quarters.

Establishing personal Sabbat traditions will help you grow and attune to the rhythms of the seasons. Your traditions create comforting anchors for your mind and spirit. You might prepare a special recipe every Yule, harvest magical herbs every Midsummer, or make candles every Imbolc. Explore the seasonal activities you enjoy, and incorporate them into your tradition.

Quarters

The four Quarter Sabbats are the two solstices and two equinoxes. These astrological events do not occur on the same day every year. The Quarter Sabbats divide the earth's path around the sun (the ecliptic) into quarters, falling 90° apart on the ecliptic.

Cross-Quarters

The four Cross-Quarters are traditional Sabbats that are celebrated at the same time every year. Their dates do not fall exactly halfway between the Quarter Sabbats. They include Imbolc (Feb. 1–2), Beltane (Apr. 30–May 1), Lughnasadh or Lammas (Aug. 1–2), and Samhain (Oct. 31–Nov. 1).

Exact Astronomical Cross-Quarters

The exact astronomical Cross-Quarter Sabbats occur when the earth is precisely halfway along the ecliptic between a solstice and an equinox. The Quarters and astronomical Cross Quarters are 45° apart on the ecliptic.

Many witches combine the traditional Cross-Quarter Sabbat dates with the astronomical Cross-Quarters. For example, traditional Samhain celebrations begin on October 31st and continue through November 1st. The astronomical Cross-Quarter date for Samhain is November 6th, and some witches celebrate Samhain from October 31st through November 6th.

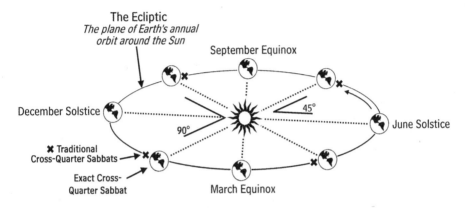

Traditional Cross-Quarter Sabbats are shown with ✘ and are just before the astronomical Cross-Quarters.

Northern & Southern Hemispheres

The Sabbat you celebrate on a particular date depends on your tradition and location. Witches in the Southern Hemisphere (SH) often learn their craft from materials written for the Northern Hemisphere (NH). These SH witches may observe the same Sabbats simultaneously as witches in the NH. However, SH witches sometimes choose to celebrate according to the local seasons. Rather than celebrate Beltane on May 1st, when it is autumn in the Southern Hemisphere, these witches may reverse the Sabbats and observe Samhain. Then on October 31st, they celebrate Beltane.

Remember, you are the authority in your practice!
You have the final say in which Sabbats you observe,
when you celebrate, and what names you use for them.

THE FULL MOONS OF 2025

Jan 13
4:26 pm
♋

Feb 12
7:53 am
♌

Mar 14
1:54 am
♍

Apr 12
7:21 pm
♎

May 12
11:55 am
♏

Jun 11
2:43 am
♐

Jul 10
3:36 pm
♑

Aug 9
2:54 am
♒

Sep 7
1:08 pm
♓

Oct 6
10:47 pm
♈

Nov 5
7:19 am
♉

Dec 4
5:13 pm
♊

Notable Full Moon Events

Total Lunar Eclipse: March 14
Micro Full Moon: April 12, May 12
Super Full Moon: November 5, December 4

January Lunar Planner

M	T	W	T	F	S	S
		1	2	3	4	5
6	7	8	9	10	11	12
13	14	15	16	17	18	19
20	21	22	23	24	25	26
27	28	29	30	31		

National Blood Donor Month
National Braille Literacy Month
National Hobby Month
National Hot Tea Month

We	1	● US★
Th	2	●
Fr	3	● ◑ 6:33 am
Sa	4	◐
Su	5	◐
Mo	6	◐ ◑ 5:56 pm
Tu	7	◑
We	8	◑
Th	9	◯
Fr	10	◯ ○ 4:19 am
Sa	11	◯
Su	12	◯

Mo 13 ○ ○ 4:26 pm

Tu 14 ○

We 15 ○

Th 16 ○

Fr 17 ◐ ☽ 11:35 am

Sa 18 ◐

Su 19 ◐ ☉→♒ 2:00 pm

Mo 20 ◑ US★

Tu 21 ◑ ☽ 2:30 pm

We 22 ◑

Th 23 ◑

Fr 24 ◑

Sa 25 ◕ ☽ 3:12 pm

Su 26 ◕

Mo 27 ◕

Tu 28 ●

We 29 ● ● 6:35 am

Th 30 ●

Fr 31 ●

February Lunar Planner

February

M	T	W	T	F	S	S
					1	2
3	4	5	6	7	8	9
10	11	12	13	14	15	16
17	18	19	20	21	22	23
24	25	26	27	28		

Black History Month
Library Lovers Month
Great American Pie Month

Sa 1 ◗ ◗ 4:20 pm   ✿

Su 2 ◗

Mo 3 ◗   ⊗

Tu 4 ◗

We 5 ◐ ◐ 2:01 am

Th 6 ◐

Fr 7 ◐

Sa 8 ○ ○ 2:31 pm

Su 9 ○

Mo 10 ○

Tu 11 ○

We 12 ○ ○ 7:53 am

Th	13	◯	
Fr	14	◯	
Sa	15	◯	
Su	16	◯	☾ 8:08 am
Mo	17	◯	US★
Tu	18	◐	☉→♓ 4:07 am
We	19	◐	
Th	20	◐	◑ 11:32 am
Fr	21	◐	
Sa	22	◐	
Su	23	◐	
Mo	24	◐	◑ 8:04 am
Tu	25	◐	
We	26	◑	
Th	27	●	● 6:44 pm
Fr	28	●	

Theban Script

ᚠ	ᚢ	ᚦ	ᚩ	ᚱ	ᚳ	ᚷ	ᚹ	ᚻ	ᚾ	ᛁ	ᛄ
A	B	C	D	E	F	G	H	I/J	K	L	M

ᛟ	ᛝ	ᛞ	ᛖ	ᛗ	ᛘ	ᛙ	ᛚ	ᛛ	ᛜ	ᛠ	ᛡ
N	O	P	Q	R	S	T	U/V	W	X	Y	Z

March Lunar Planner

M	T	W	T	F	S	S
					1	2
3	4	5	6	7	8	9
10	11	12	13	14	15	16
17	18	19	20	21	22	23
24	25	26	27	28	29	30
31						

National Craft Month
Women's History Month
National Nutrition Month
National Women's History Month

Sa 1

Su 2

Mo 3 ◑ 1:16 am

Tu 4

We 5

Th 6 ◑ 10:31 am

Fr 7

Sa 8

Su 9

Mo 10 ○ 3:19 am

Tu 11

We 12

Th	13	○	
Fr	14	○	○ 1:54 am
Sa	15	○	
Su	16	○	
Mo	17	○	
Tu	18	○	◑ 5:00 am
We	19	◐	
Th	20	◐	✤ ⊙→♈ 4:01am
Fr	21	◐	
Sa	22	◐	◑ 6:29 am
Su	23	◐	
Mo	24	◐	
Tu	25	◖	◕ 10:48 pm
We	26	●	
Th	27	●	
Fr	28	●	
Sa	29	●	● 5:57 am
Su	30	●	
Mo	31	●	

April Lunar Planner

M	T	W	T	F	S	S
	1	2	3	4	5	6
7	8	9	10	11	12	13
14	15	16	17	18	19	20
21	22	23	24	25	26	27
28	29	30				

National Garden Month
Child Abuse Prevention Month
National Autism Awareness Month
Sexual Assault Awareness Month

Tu   1   ◑   ◐ 10:47 am

We   2   ◑

Th   3   ◑

Fr   4   ◑   ◐ 9:14 pm

Sa   5   ◐

Su   6   ◖

Mo   7   ◖

Tu   8   ◖   ○ 5:06 pm

We   9   ◯

Th 10   ◯

Fr 11   ◯

Sa 12   ◯   ○ 7:21 pm

Su 13   ◯

Mo 14 ○

Tu 15 ○

We 16 ○ ◐ 10:23 pm

Th 17 ○

Fr 18 ○

Sa 19 ○ ☉→♉ 2:56 pm

Su 20 ◐ ◑ 8:35 pm

Mo 21 ◐

Tu 22 ◐

We 23 ◐

Th 24 ◑ ◑ 9:23 am

Fr 25 ◑

Sa 26 ●

Su 27 ● ● 2:30pm

Mo 28 ●

Tu 29 ●

We 30 ● ◕ 7:32 pm

May Lunar Planner

M	T	W	T	F	S	S
			1	2	3	4
5	6	7	8	9	10	11
12	13	14	15	16	17	18
19	20	21	22	23	24	25
26	27	28	29	30	31	

National Bike Month
Mental Health Awareness Month
National Stroke Awareness Month

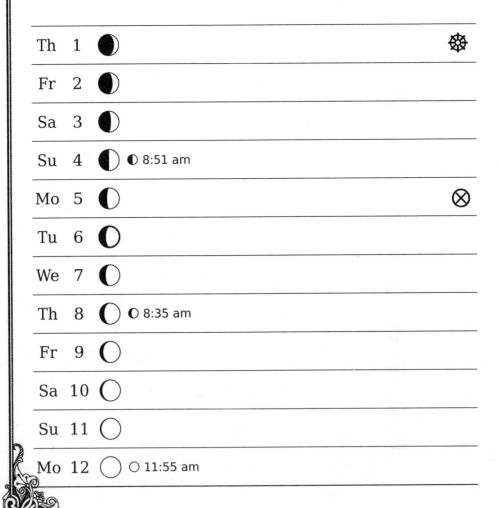

Th   1   🌓   ✸

Fr   2   🌓

Sa   3   🌓

Su   4   🌓   ◑ 8:51 am

Mo   5   🌗   ⊗

Tu   6   🌑

We   7   🌑

Th   8   🌘   ◐ 8:35 am

Fr   9   🌘

Sa 10   🌘

Su 11   🌘

Mo 12   🌕   ○ 11:55 am

Tu 13 ○

We 14 ○

Th 15 ○

Fr 16 ○   ☽ 12:28 pm

Sa 17 ○

Su 18 ○

Mo 19 ○

Tu 20 ◐   �� 6:58 am, ☉→Ⅱ 1:55 pm

We 21 ◐

Th 22 ◐

Fr 23 ◖   ◑ 5:14 pm

Sa 24 ◖

Su 25 ●

Mo 26 ●   ● 10:02 pm   US★

Tu 27 ●

We 28 ●

Th 29 ◗

Fr 30 ◗   ◐ 5:17 am

Sa 31 ◗

June Lunar Planner

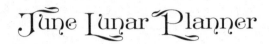

M	T	W	T	F	S	S
						1
2	3	4	5	6	7	8
9	10	11	12	13	14	15
16	17	18	19	20	21	22
23	24	25	26	27	28	29
30						

Rose Month
LGBTQIA+ Pride Month
National Adopt a Cat Month
National Candy Month

Su   1

Mo   2

Tu   3   ◑ 10:40 pm

We   4

Th   5

Fr   6

Sa   7   ○ 12:56 am

Su   8

Mo   9

Tu   10

We   11   ○ 2:43 am

Th   12

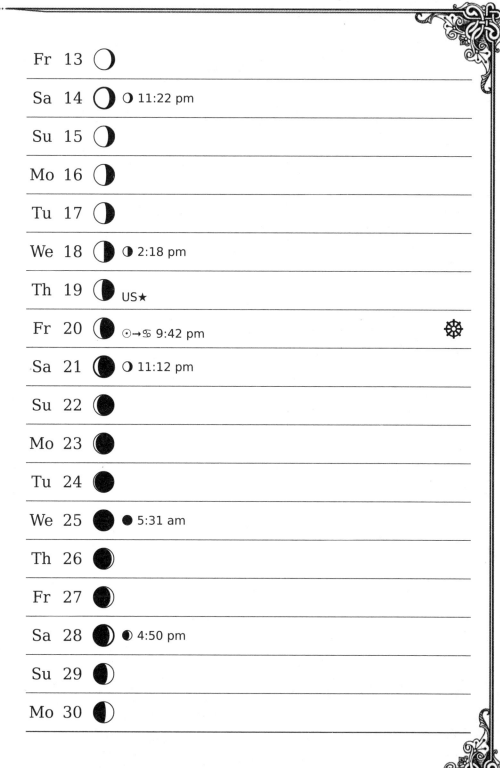

Fr	13		
Sa	14	☽	11:22 pm
Su	15		
Mo	16		
Tu	17		
We	18	◑	2:18 pm
Th	19	US★	
Fr	20	☉→♋	9:42 pm
Sa	21	☽	11:12 pm
Su	22		
Mo	23		
Tu	24		
We	25	●	5:31 am
Th	26		
Fr	27		
Sa	28	◐	4:50 pm
Su	29		
Mo	30		

July Lunar Planner

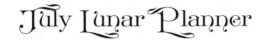

M	T	W	T	F	S	S
	1	2	3	4	5	6
7	8	9	10	11	12	13
14	15	16	17	18	19	20
21	22	23	24	25	26	27
28	29	30	31			

Disability Pride Month
National Ice Cream Month
National Picnic Month

Tu 1 ◗

We 2 ◗ ◑ 2:29 pm

Th 3 ◖

Fr 4 ◖ US★

Sa 5 ◖

Su 6 ◖ ◐ 5:16 pm

Mo 7 ○

Tu 8 ○

We 9 ○

Th 10 ○ ○ 3:36 pm

Fr 11 ○

Sa 12 ○

Su 13 ◗

Mo 14 ◗ ◐ 7:47 am

Tu 15 ◗

We 16 ◖

Th 17 ◖ ◑ 7:37 pm

Fri 18 ◖

Sa 19 ◖

Su 20 ◖

Mo 21 ◖ ◕ 4:30 am

Tu 22 ◖ ☉→♌ 8:30 am

We 23 ●

Th 24 ● ● 2:10 pm

Fr 25 ●

Sa 26 ●

Su 27 ●

Mo 28 ◗ ◑ 6:40 am

Tu 29 ◗

We 30 ◗

Th 31 ◗

Aυgυst Lυŋar Plaŋŋer

M	T	W	T	F	S	S
				1	2	3
4	5	6	7	8	9	10
11	12	13	14	15	16	17
18	19	20	21	22	23	24
25	26	27	28	29	30	31

Black Business Month
National Picnic Month
National Back to School Month
International Peace Month

Fr 1   ◑ ◐ 7:41 am   ✵

Sa 2   ◑

Su 3   ◑

Mo 4   ◑

Tu 5   ◑ ◐ 8:59 am

We 6   ◑

Th 7   ◯   ⊗

Fr 8   ◯

Sa 9   ◯ ○ 2:54 am

Su 10   ◯

Mo 11   ◯

Tu 12   ◯ ○ 2:38 pm

We	13	◗	
Th	14	◗	
Fr	15	◗	
Sa	16	◗	◖ 12:11 am
Su	17	◖	
Mo	18	◖	
Tu	19	◖	◑ 10:37 am
We	20	◖	
Th	21	◖	
Fr	22	●	☉→♍ 3:34 pm
Sa	23	●	● 1:06 am
Su	24	●	
Mo	25	●	
Tu	26	◗	◑ 10:44 pm
We	27	◗	
Th	28	◗	
Fr	29	◗	
Sa	30	◗	
Su	31	◗	◐ 1:24 am

September Lunar Planner

M	T	W	T	F	S	S
1	2	3	4	5	6	7
8	9	10	11	12	13	14
15	16	17	18	19	20	21
22	23	24	25	26	27	28
29	30					

National Mushroom Month
Suicide Prevention Month
Self Improvement Month

Mo 1 ◐ US★

Tu 2 ◐

We 3 ◐ ○ 11:52 pm

Th 4 ○

Fr 5 ○

Sa 6 ○

Su 7 ○ ○ 1:08 pm

Mo 8 ○

Tu 9 ○

We 10 ○ ○ 8:58 pm

Th 11 ◑

Fr 12 ◑

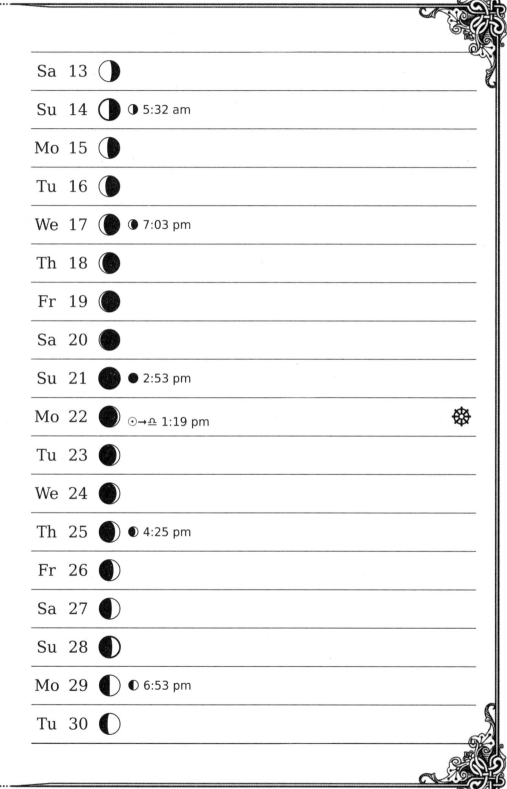

Sa	13	
Su	14	◑ 5:32 am
Mo	15	
Tu	16	
We	17	◐ 7:03 pm
Th	18	
Fr	19	
Sa	20	
Su	21	● 2:53 pm
Mo	22	☉→♎ 1:19 pm
Tu	23	
We	24	
Th	25	◐ 4:25 pm
Fr	26	
Sa	27	
Su	28	
Mo	29	◑ 6:53 pm
Tu	30	

October Lunar Planner

M	T	W	T	F	S	S
		1	2	3	4	5
6	7	8	9	10	11	12
13	14	15	16	17	18	19
20	21	22	23	24	25	26
27	28	29	30	31		

National Book Month
National Apple Month
Bat Appreciation Month
LGBTQIA+ History Month
Breast Cancer Awareness Month

We 1 ◗

Th 2 ◗

Fri 3 ◗ ☉ 1:46 pm

Sa 4 ◖

Su 5 ◖

Mo 6 ◯ ○ 10:47 pm

Tu 7 ◯

We 8 ◯

Th 9 ◖

Fr 10 ◗ ☉ 3:56 am

Sa 11 ◗

Su 12 ◗

Mo 13 ◑ ◑ 1:12 pm   US ★

Tu 14 ◑

We 15 ◑

Th 16 ◑

Fr 17 ◑ ◕ 6:56 am

Sa 18 ●

Su 19 ●

Mo 20 ●

Tu 21 ● ● 7:24 am

We 22 ● ☉→♏ 10:51 pm

Th 23 ●

Fr 24 ●

Sa 25 ◐ ◑ 10:42 am

Su 26 ◐

Mo 27 ◐

Tu 28 ◐

We 29 ◐ ◑ 11:20 am

Th 30 ◑

Fr 31 ◯   ✿

November Lunar Planner

M	T	W	T	F	S	S
					1	2
3	4	5	6	7	8	9
10	11	12	13	14	15	16
17	18	19	20	21	22	23
24	25	26	27	28	29	30

Native American Heritage Month
Gratitude Month
Diabetes Month

Sa　1　◗

Su　2　◗　◔ 1:29 am

Mo　3　◗

Tu　4　◗

We　5　◯　○ 7:19 am

Th　6　◗　　　　　　　　　　　　⊗

Fr　7　◗

Sa　8　◖　◑ 11:39 am

Su　9　◖

Mo　10　◖

Tu　11　◖　◑ 11:27 pm　　　　　US★

We　12　◖

Th	13	◑
Fr	14	◑
Sa	15	◑ ◑ 9:38 pm
Su	16	◑
Mo	17	●
Tu	18	●
We	19	●
Th	20	● ● 12:46 am
Fr	21	● ☉→♐ 7:36 pm
Sa	22	●
Su	23	●
Mo	24	● ◑ 3:24 am
Tu	25	◐
We	26	◐
Th	27	◐ US★
Fr	28	◐ ◑ 12:58 am
Sa	29	◯
Su	30	◯

December Lunar Planner

M	T	W	T	F	S	S
1	2	3	4	5	6	7
8	9	10	11	12	13	14
15	16	17	18	19	20	21
22	23	24	25	26	27	28
29	30	31				

Human Rights Month
Spiritual Literacy Month
Read a New Book Month

Mo 1 ◑ ○ 12:48 am

Tu 2 ◑

We 3 ◑

Th 4 ◯ ○ 5:13 pm

Fr 5 ◯

Sa 6 ◯

Su 7 ◑ ◐ 11:04 pm

Mo 8 ◑

Tu 9 ◑

We 10 ◑

Th 11 ◑ ◐ 2:51 pm

Fr 12 ◑

Sa	13	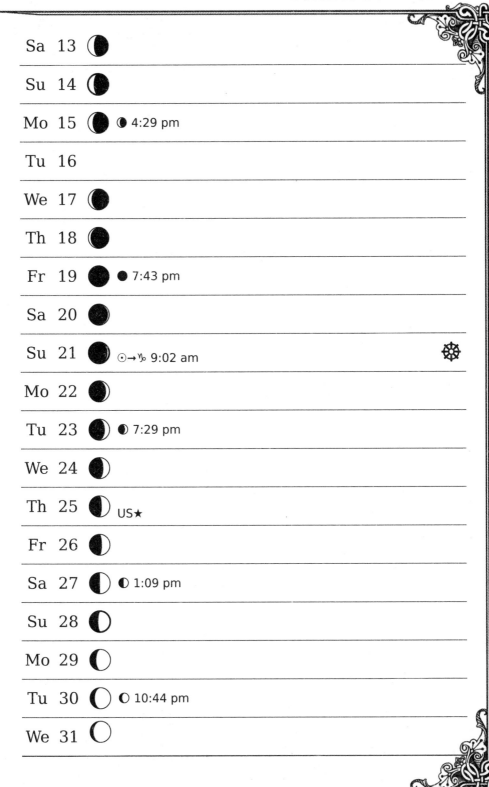	
Su	14		
Mo	15	☾ 4:29 pm	
Tu	16		
We	17		
Th	18		
Fr	19	● 7:43 pm	
Sa	20		
Su	21	☉→♑ 9:02 am	✲
Mo	22		
Tu	23	☽ 7:29 pm	
We	24		
Th	25	US★	
Fr	26		
Sa	27	☽ 1:09 pm	
Su	28		
Mo	29		
Tu	30	☽ 10:44 pm	
We	31		

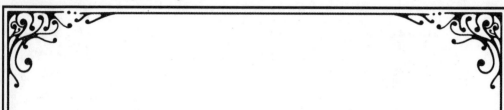

Monday, December 30, 2024

● ♑ 4:26 pm (Black Moon)

Good time for banishing.

Tuesday 31

⚹ ♄ 1:02 am
New Year's Eve

Wednesday, January 1, 2025

☽→♒ 4:50 am
US★ New Year's Day

Thursday 2

✳☿ 8:33 pm

National Science Fiction Day

Friday 3

)→♓ 9:21 am
● 6:33 am
☄ Quadrantids

Saturday 4

☄ Quadrantids
Perihelion 7:28 am

National Trivia Day

Sunday 5

□☿ 5:57 am
)→♈ 1:01 pm

National Whipped Cream Day

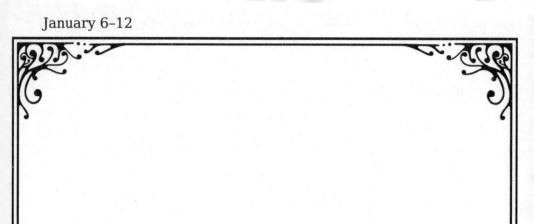

Monday 6

◑ 5:56 pm

National Cuddle Up Day

Tuesday 7

□♂ 3:15 pm
)→♉ *4:12 pm*

Wednesday 8

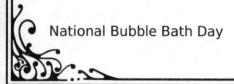

National Bubble Bath Day

Thursday 9

✳♂ 4:49 pm
☽→♊ 7:07 pm

Friday 10

◖ 4:19 am
☐♄ 9:15 pm

National Houseplant Appreciation Day
See Venus near the western horizon just after sunset.

Saturday 11

☽→♋ 10:24 pm

National Human Trafficking Awareness Day

Sunday 12

Monday 13

○ 4:26 pm

Korean American Day

Tuesday 14

☽→♌ 3:12 am

Wednesday 15

✳︎♃ 12:58 am

National Hat Day

 Thursday 16

    ☽→♍ 10:46 am

National Nothing Day
Mars is close and at opposition—this
may be a good night to view the planet.

Friday 17

    ◑ 11:35 am

Saturday 18

    △☉ 8:00 pm
    ☽→♎ 9:33 pm

World Religion Day

Sunday 19

    ☉→♒ 2:00 pm

 National Popcorn Day

Monday 20

US★ Martin Luther King Jr. Day
□♂ 10:33 pm

Tuesday 21

☽→♏ 10:20 am
◑ 2:30 pm

National Hugging Day

Wednesday 22

Thursday 23

△♂9:12 am
☽→♐ 10:29 pm

Friday 24

National Compliment Day

Saturday 25

☽ 3:12 pm
□♀ 10:24 pm

Opposite Day

Sunday 26

☽→♑ &:43 am

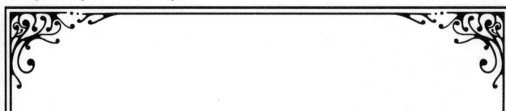

Monday 27

International Holocaust Remembrance Day

Tuesday 28

⚹♀ 3:52 am
☽→♒ 1:32 pm

National Lego Day

Wednesday 29

● 6:35 am
△♃ 9:08 am

Lunar New Year
(Year of the Green Wood Snake begins)

Thursday 30

)→)(4:53 pm

Friday 31

National Hot Chocolate Day

Saturday 1

♂♀ 4:05 pm
◗ 4:20 pm
)→♈ 7:10 pm
❀ Imbolc/Lughnasadh

National Freedom Day

Sunday 2

Monday 3 ⊗

□♂ 4:19 am
☽→♉ 9:34 pm
⊗ 8:02 am

National Carrot Cake Day
National Women Physicians Day

Tuesday 4

Rosa Parks Day

Wednesday 5

☽ 2:01 am
✶♂ 6:16 am

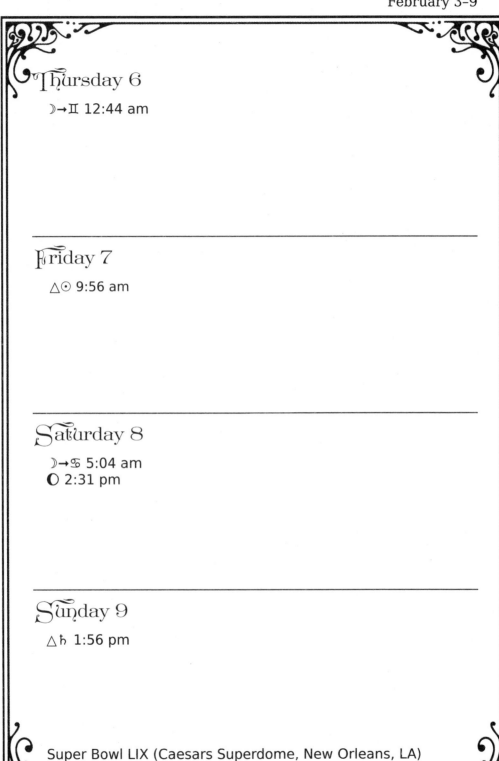

Thursday 6
☽→♊ 12:44 am

Friday 7
△☉ 9:56 am

Saturday 8
☽→♋ 5:04 am
☽ 2:31 pm

Sunday 9
△♄ 1:56 pm

Super Bowl LIX (Caesars Superdome, New Orleans, LA)

Monday 10

)→♌ 11:01 am

Tuesday 11

National Inventors' Day
International Day of Women and Girls in Science

Wednesday 12

○ 7:53 am
☍☿ 1:11 pm
)→♍ 7:07 pm

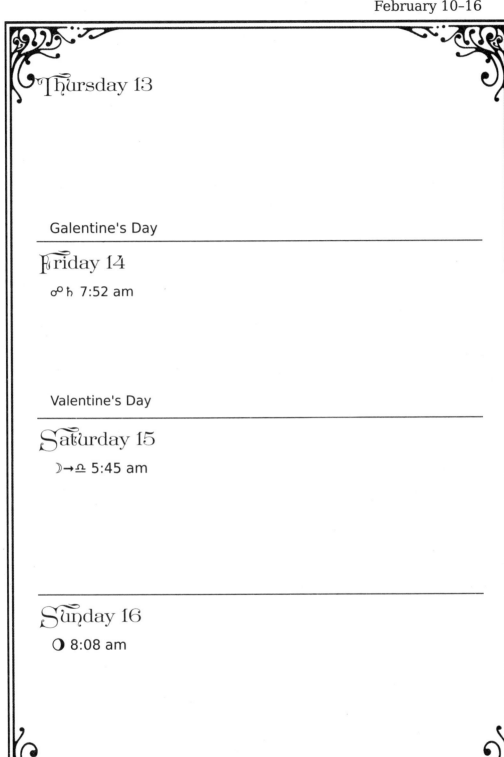

Thursday 13

Galentine's Day

Friday 14

☍ ♄ 7:52 am

Valentine's Day

Saturday 15

☽→♎ 5:45 am

Sunday 16

◑ 8:08 am

Monday 17

△☉ 5:23 pm
☽→♏ 6:19 pm

US★ Presidents' Day

Tuesday 18

☉→♓ 4:07 am

Wednesday 19

△♄ 9:58 am

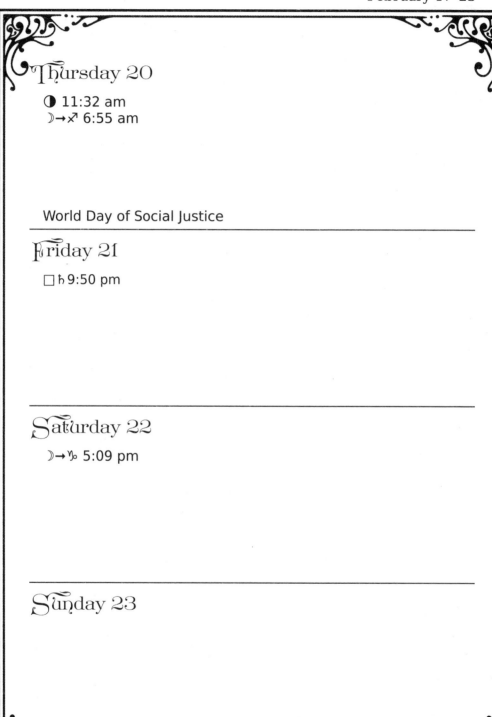

Thursday 20

◑ 11:32 am
☽→♐ 6:55 am

World Day of Social Justice

Friday 21

□ ♄ 9:50 pm

Saturday 22

☽→♑ 5:09 pm

Sunday 23

M︠o︠n︠day 24

✶ ♄ 6:09 am
◑ 8:04 am
☽→♒ 11:40 pm

T︠u︠esday 25

△ ♃ 8:32 pm

W︠e︠d︠nesday 26

Thursday 27

)→⯑ 2:47 am
● 6:44 pm

Friday 28

♂♀ 10:18 pm

Saturday 1

)→♈ 3:52 am

Zero Discrimination Day

Sunday 2

□♂ 7:51 am

Read Across America

Monday 3

● 1:16 am
☽→♉ 4:37 am

World Wildlife Day

Tuesday 4

⚹♄ 3:36 pm
Mardi Gras

Wednesday 5

☽→♊ 6:30 am

Thursday 6

◑ 10:31 am
□ ♄ 7:22 pm
Dred Scott Case, 1857

Friday 7

☽→♋ 10:29 am

National Day of Unplugging

Saturday 8

International Women's Day
Mercury is low on western horizon after sunset tonight.

Sunday 9

△ ♄ 1:40 am
☽→♌ 5:59 pm

Daylight Saving Time begins

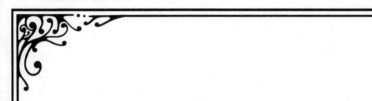

Monday 10

☽ 3:19 am
⁎ ♃ 6:45 pm

Harriet Tubman Day

Tuesday 11

Wednesday 12

☽→♍ 2:56 am

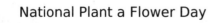

National Plant a Flower Day

Thursday 13

National Popcorn Lovers Day

Friday 14

♂☌☉ 1:54 am
)→♎ 1:39 pm
○ 1:54 am
Total Lunar Eclipse

π Pi Day

Saturday 15

☿℞ Begins

Sunday 16

□♂ 4:52 am

Monday 17

☽→♏ 2:31 am

Saint Patrick's Day

Tuesday 18

☾ 5:00 am

Awkward Moments Day

Wednesday 19

△☉ 2:07 pm
☽→♐ 3:17 pm

 ## Thursday 20

❀ 4:01 am Equinox
Ostara/Mabon
☉→♈ 4:01am

Friday 21

□ ♄ 1:23 pm

International Day of Forests

Saturday 22

☽→♑ 2:29 am
◑ 6:29 am

Sunday 23

∗ ♄ 10:41 pm

 National Puppy Day

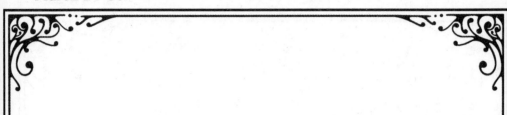

Monday 24

☽→♒ 10:25 am

Tuesday 25

△♃ 1:00 pm
● 10:48 pm

International Waffle Day

Wednesday 26

☽→♓ 2:32 pm

**Thursday 27**

World Theater Day

Friday 28

♂♀ 2:16 pm
☽→♈ 3:36 pm

Emotional Awareness

Saturday 29

● 5:57 am
Partial Solar Eclipse

Earth Hour (Power down electrical use 8:30 pm - 9:30 pm)

**Sunday 30**

□♂ 4:17 am
☽→♉ 3:16 pm

Monday 31

Trans Day Of Visibility

Tuesday 1

◗ 10:47 am
✳☿ 12:42 pm
☽→♊ 3:26 pm

April Fool's Day

Wednesday 2

Autism Awareness Day

Thursday 3

□☿ 1:26 pm
☽→♋ 5:50 pm

National Rainbow Day

Friday 4

◑ 9:14 pm

Saturday 5

△☿ 5:54 pm
☽→♌ 11:34 pm

National Dandelion Day

Sunday 6

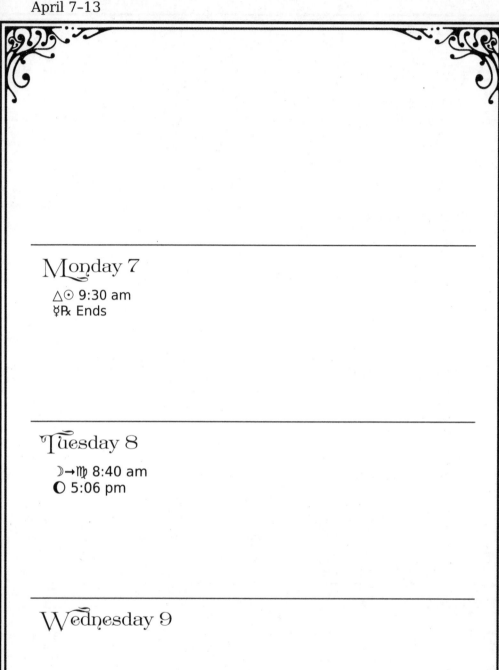

Monday 7

△☉ 9:30 am
☿℞ Ends

Tuesday 8

☽→♍ 8:40 am
◗ 5:06 pm

Wednesday 9

National Name Yourself Day

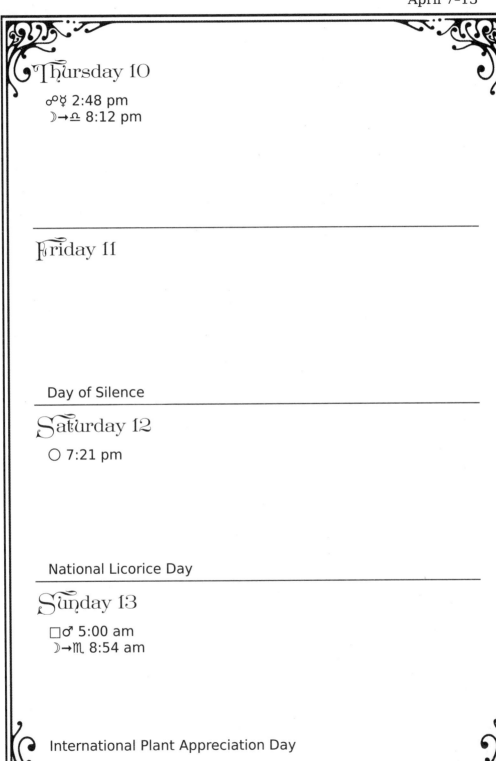

Thursday 10

☍☿ 2:48 pm
☽→♎ 8:12 pm

Friday 11

Day of Silence

Saturday 12

○ 7:21 pm

National Licorice Day

Sunday 13

□♂ 5:00 am
☽→♏ 8:54 am

International Plant Appreciation Day

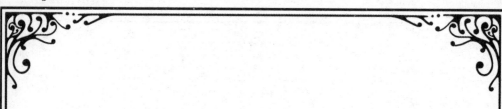

Monday 14

National Gardening Day

Tuesday 15

△☿ 9:23 pm
☽→♐ 9:37 pm

Tax Day

Wednesday 16

☾ 10:23 pm

Thursday 17

International Bat Appreciation Day

Friday 18

△☉6:37 am
☽→♑ 9:12 am

Saturday 19

☉→♉ 2:56 pm

Sunday 20

◑ 8:35 pm
✳ ♄ 12:20 pm
☽→♒ 6:22 pm

Monday 21

Mercury is low in the eastern sky just before sunrise.

Tuesday 22

△♃ 6:04 am
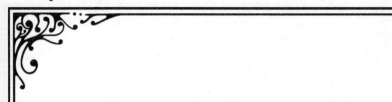 Lyrids

Earth Day

Wednesday 23

☽→♓ 12:07 am
 Lyrids

National Talk Like Shakespeare Day

Thursday 24

◑ 9:23 am
♂♀ 9:57 pm

Friday 25

☽→♈ 2:24 am

Saturday 26

⚹♃ 11:17 am

Sunday 27

● 2:30pm
☽→♉ 2:17 am

Monday 28

Tuesday 29

✳♀ 12:17 am
☽→♊ 1:35 am

International Dance Day

Wednesday 30

□♄ 10:48 pm
◐ 7:32 pm

 Thursday 1

)→♋ 2:23 am
✳ Beltane/Samhain

Friday 2

National Space Day

Saturday 3

△♄ 3:01 am
)→♌ 6:29 am
⛤

World Press Freedom Day
Transformation & Action

Sunday 4

⚹♃ 11:43 pm
◑ 8:51 am

May the 4th be with you.

Monday 5 ⊗

)→♍ 12:40 pm
⊗ 12:49 am

International Day of the Midwife

Tuesday 6

Eta Aquarids

International No Diet Day

Wednesday 7

☍ ♄ 11:10 pm
Eta Aquarids

Thursday 8

☽→♎ 2:07 am
🌑 8:35 am

Friday 9

National Lost Sock Memorial Day

Saturday 10

△♃ 1:17 am
☽→♏ 12:59 pm

Sunday 11

Mother's Day

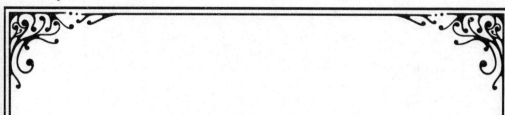

Monday 12

○ 11:55 am

National Limerick Day

Tuesday 13

△♄ 1:36 am
)→♐ 3:35 am

Wednesday 14

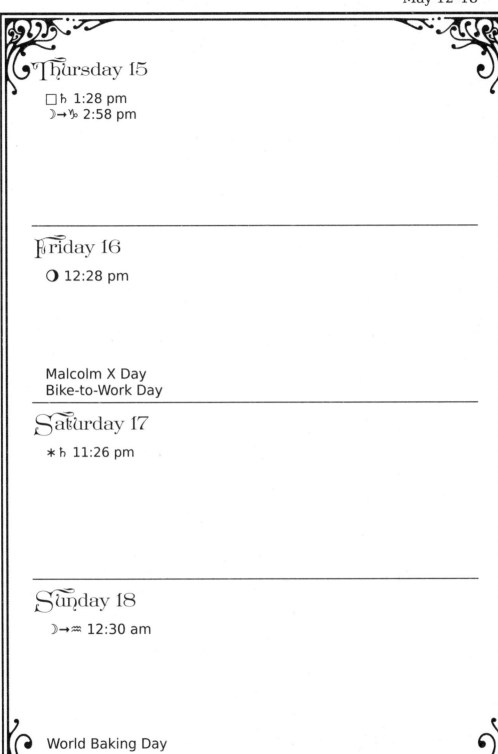

Thursday 15

☐ ♄ 1:28 pm
☽→♑ 2:58 pm

Friday 16

☽ 12:28 pm

Malcolm X Day
Bike-to-Work Day

Saturday 17

⁎ ♄ 11:26 pm

Sunday 18

☽→♒ 12:30 am

World Baking Day

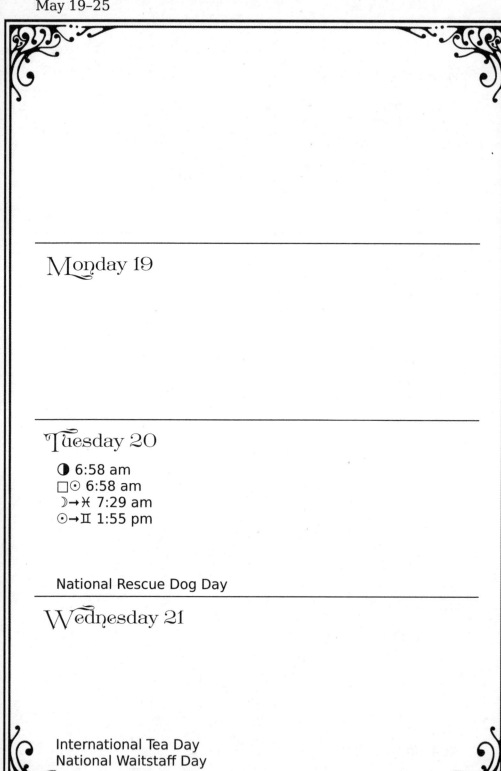

Monday 19

Tuesday 20

◑ 6:58 am
□☉ 6:58 am
☽→♓ 7:29 am
☉→♊ 1:55 pm

National Rescue Dog Day

Wednesday 21

International Tea Day
National Waitstaff Day

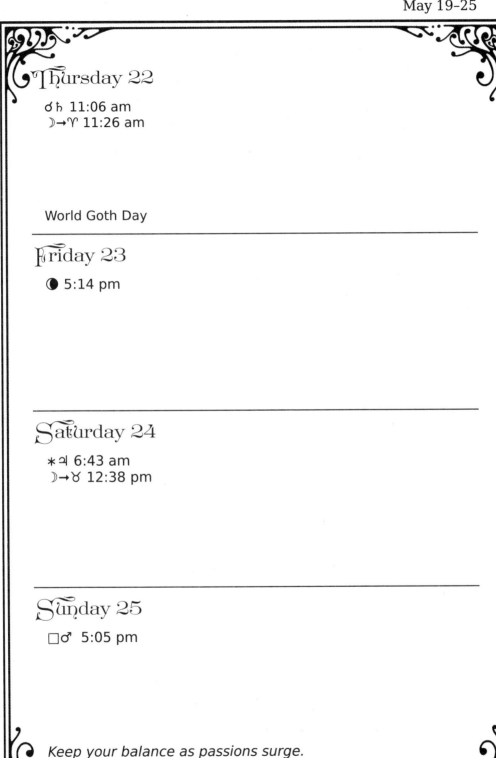

Thursday 22

☌ ♄ 11:06 am
☽→♈ 11:26 am

World Goth Day

Friday 23

◑ 5:14 pm

Saturday 24

⚹ ♃ 6:43 am
☽→♉ 12:38 pm

Sunday 25

□ ♂ 5:05 pm

Keep your balance as passions surge.

Monday 26

● 10:02 pm
☽→♊ 12:22 pm

US★ Memorial Day

Tuesday 27

National Sunscreen Day

Wednesday 28

♂♌ 8:00 am
☽→♋ 12:33 pm

Thursday 29

Learn About Composting Day

Friday 30

◗ 5:17 am
□♀ 3:44 am
☽→♌ 3:17 pm

Saturday 31

Venus is low on the eastern horizon just before sunrise.

Sunday 1

✳♃ 6:37 pm
☽→♍ 10:00 pm

Monday 2

◑ 10:40 pm

Tuesday 3

World Bicycle Day

Wednesday 4

□♃ 6:11 am
☽→♎ 8:39 am

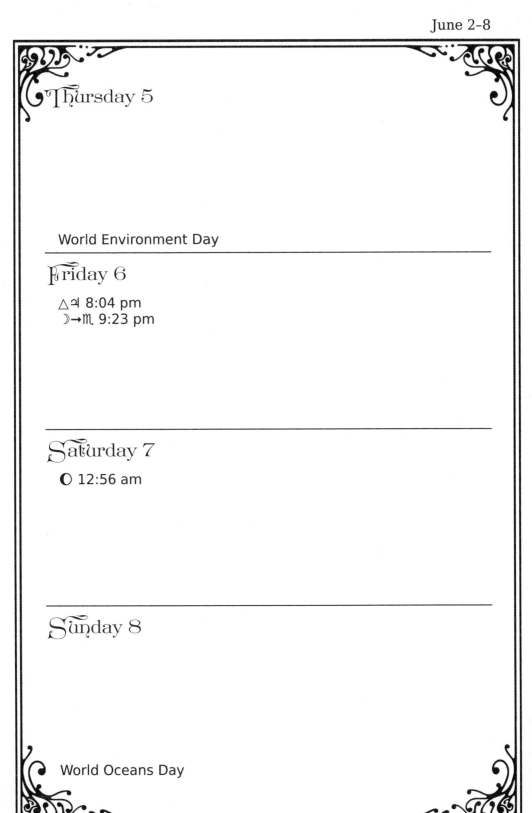

Thursday 5

World Environment Day

Friday 6

△ ♃ 8:04 pm
☽→♏ 9:23 pm

Saturday 7

◖ 12:56 am

Sunday 8

World Oceans Day

Monday 9

□♂ 12:56 am
☽→♐ 9:56 am

Tuesday 10

National Iced Tea Day

Wednesday 11

○ 2:43 am
△♂ 12:57 pm
☽→♑ 8:55 pm

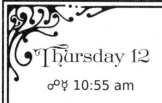

Thursday 12

☌☿ 10:55 am

World Day Against Child Labor
Balance emotions with reason through reflection.

Friday 13

Saturday 14

☽→♒ 6:00 am
◖ 11:22 pm

World Blood Donor Day

Sunday 15

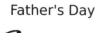

Father's Day

Monday 16

☌♂ 12:30 pm
☽→♓ 1:09 pm

National Fudge Day

Tuesday 17

Wednesday 18

☾ 2:18 pm
□☉ 2:18 pm
☽→♈ 6:08 pm

International Picnic Day

 **Thursday 19**

US★ Juneteenth

Friday 20

✳☉ 8:49 am
☽→♉ 8:53 pm
☉→♋ 9:42 pm
❊ 9:42 pm Solstice
    Midsummer/Yule

Take a Road Trip Day

Saturday 21

☾ 11:12 pm

Sunday 22

✳☿ 12:44 pm
☽→♊ 9:57 pm

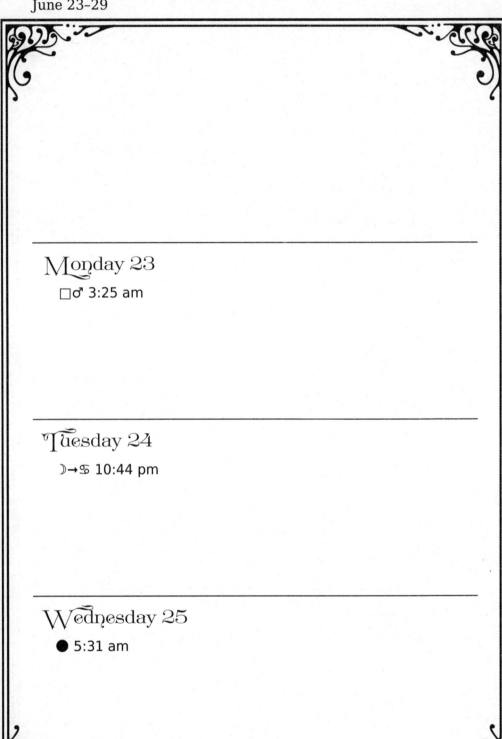

Monday 23
□♂ 3:25 am

Tuesday 24
☽→♋ 10:44 pm

Wednesday 25
● 5:31 am

Thursday 26

⚹♀ 10:07 am

Friday 27

☽→♌ 1:06 am

Helen Keller Day

Saturday 28

☽ 4:50 pm
□♀ 7:22 pm

Sunday 29

☽→♍ 6:44 am

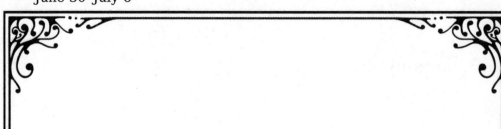

M͜ond̰ay 30

T͜uesday 1

△♀ 9:42 am
☽→♎ 4:17 pm

W͜edn̰esday 2

◐ 2:29 pm
□♂ 2:29 pm

Civil Rights Act Passed, 1964

 **Thursday 3**

Aphelion 2:54 pm

Friday 4

☽→♏ 4:33 am

US★ Independence Day
Mercury is low on the western horizon just after sunset.

Saturday 5

△☉ 8:29 am

Sunday 6

◖ 5:16 pm
☽→♐ 4:29 pm

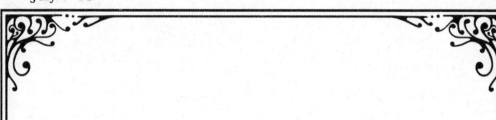

Monday 7

□♂ 4:29 pm

World Chocolate Day
Global Forgiveness Day

Tuesday 8

Wednesday 9

)→♑ 3:55 am

 Thursday 10

○ 3:36 pm
☍☉ 3:36 pm

National Kitten Day

Friday 11

☽→♒ 12:21 pm

Saturday 12

☍☿ 2:44 pm

Sunday 13

☽→♓ 6:45 pm

Monday 14
◗ 7:47 am

Tuesday 15
△☉ 12:09 pm
☽→♈ 11:33 pm

National Give Something Away Day

Wednesday 16

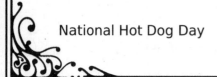

National Hot Dog Day

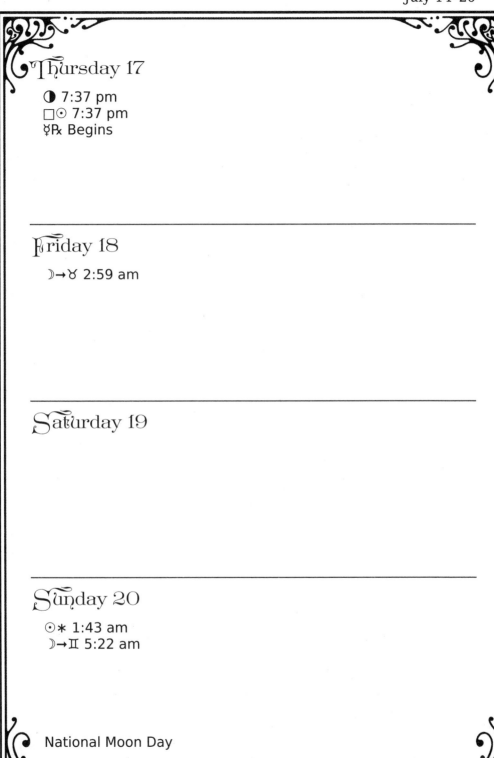

Thursday 17

◑ 7:37 pm
□☉ 7:37 pm
☿℞ Begins

Friday 18

☽→♉ 2:59 am

Saturday 19

Sunday 20

☉✳ 1:43 am
☽→♊ 5:22 am

National Moon Day

Monday 21

● 4:30 am
□♂ 2:51 pm

Tuesday 22

☽→♋ 7:26 am
☉→♌ 8:30 am

Wednesday 23

⚹♂ 7:41 pm

Thursday 24

● 2:10 pm
☽→♌ 10:29 am

Friday 25

Saturday 26

＊♀ 6:01 am
☽→♍ 3:56 pm

Sunday 27

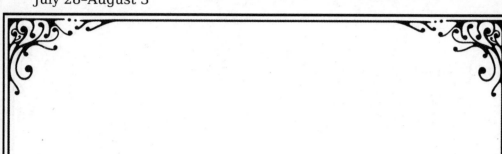

Monday 28

- ◐ 6:40 am
- □♀ 7:56 pm
- ☄ Delta Aquarids

National Milk Chocolate Day

Tuesday 29

- ☽→♎ 12:43 am
- □♃ 10:58 pm
- ☄ Delta Aquarids

Wednesday 30

International Friendship Day

Thursday 31

☽→♏ 12:25 pm

Friday 1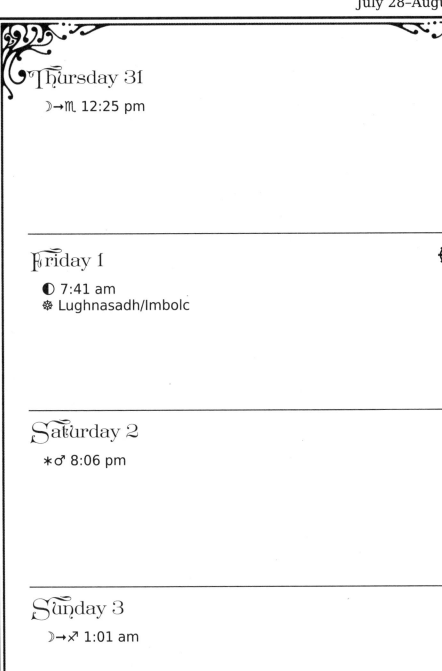

◑ 7:41 am
✾ Lughnasadh/Imbolc

Saturday 2

✱♂ 8:06 pm

Sunday 3

☽→♐ 1:01 am

National Watermelon Day

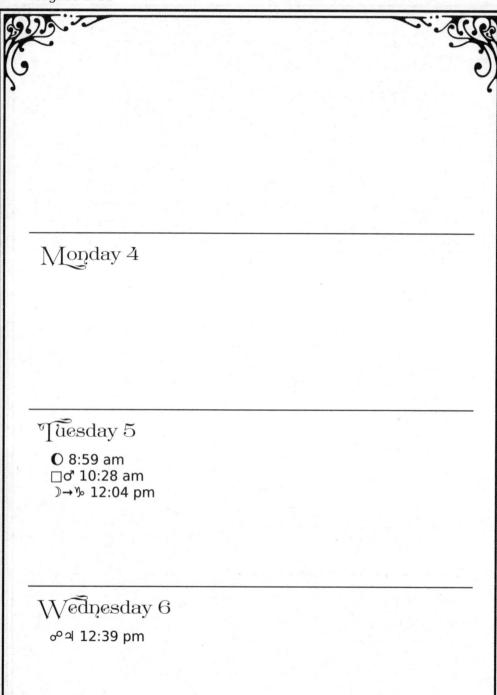

Monday 4

Tuesday 5

◐ 8:59 am
□♂ 10:28 am
☽→♑ 12:04 pm

Wednesday 6

♂°♃ 12:39 pm

Thursday 7

))→≈ 10:18 pm

Friday 8

International Cat Day

Saturday 9

○ 2:54 am
☍⊙ 2:54 am

National Book Lovers Day

Sunday 10

))→⅄ 1:50 am

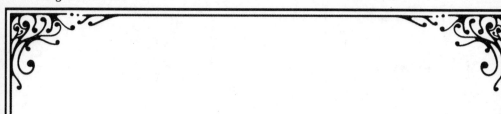

Monday 11

△♃ 1:54 am
☿℞ Ends

Tuesday 12

☽ 2:38 pm
☽→♈ 5:33 am
☄ Perseids

Wednesday 13

△☉ 5:53 pm
☄ Perseids

Left-Handers Day

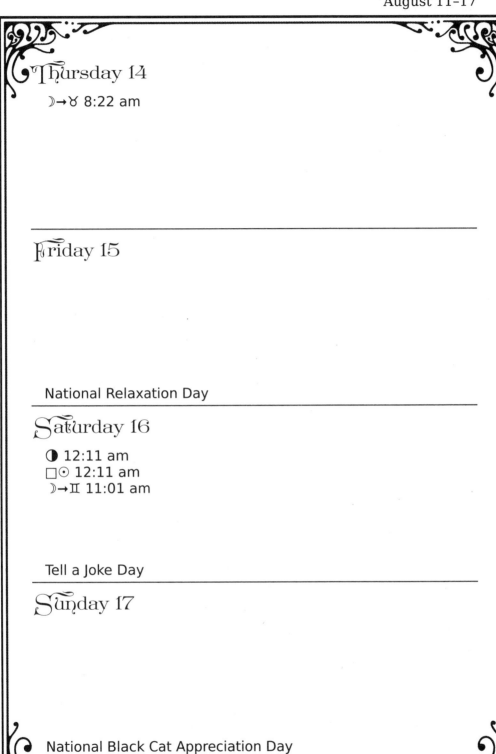

Thursday 14

)→♉ 8:22 am

Friday 15

National Relaxation Day

Saturday 16

◑ 12:11 am
□⊙ 12:11 am
)→Ⅱ 11:01 am

Tell a Joke Day

Sunday 17

National Black Cat Appreciation Day

Monday 18

✳☉ 6:52 am
☽→♋ 2:05 pm

Tuesday 19

◑ 10:37 am

*Mercury can be seen low on the
eastern horizon just before sunrise.*

Wednesday 20

♂♀ 7:26 am
☽→♌ 6:17 pm

 **Thursday 21**

♂☿ 1:13 pm

Friday 22

☉→♍ 3:34 pm

National Tooth Fairy Day

Saturday 23

● 1:06 am
☽→♍ 12:24 am

Sunday 24

National Waffle Day

Monday 25

⚹♀ 8:53 am
☽→♎ 9:08 am

Tuesday 26

◑ 10:44 pm
⚹☿ 9:06 pm

Women's Equality Day

Wednesday 27

☽→♏ 8:27 pm

Thursday 28

Friday 29

□☿ 7:46 pm

Saturday 30

☽→♐ 9:05 am

National Beach Day

Sunday 31

◑ 1:24 am

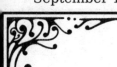

Monday 1

☐ ♄ 8:38 pm
☽→♑ 8:45 pm

US★ Labor Day

Tuesday 2

Wednesday 3

◐ 11:52 pm

Thursday 4

✳ ♄ 5:07 am
☽→♒ 5:32 am

National Wildlife Day

Friday 5

△♂ 3:51 pm

National Cheese Pizza Day

Saturday 6

☽→♓ 10:55 am

World Beard Day
Read a Book Day

Sunday 7

○ 1:08 pm
Total Lunar Eclipse

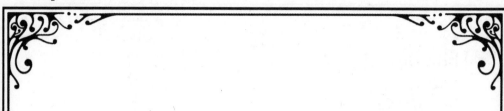

Monday 8

☌♄ 12:43 pm
☽→♈ 1:37 pm

International Literacy Day

Tuesday 9

Wednesday 10

○ 8:58 pm
☍♂ 1:53 am
☽→♉ 3:04 pm

Temporary frustrations; try to lessen with music, breathing, mindfulness, exercise, napping, etc.

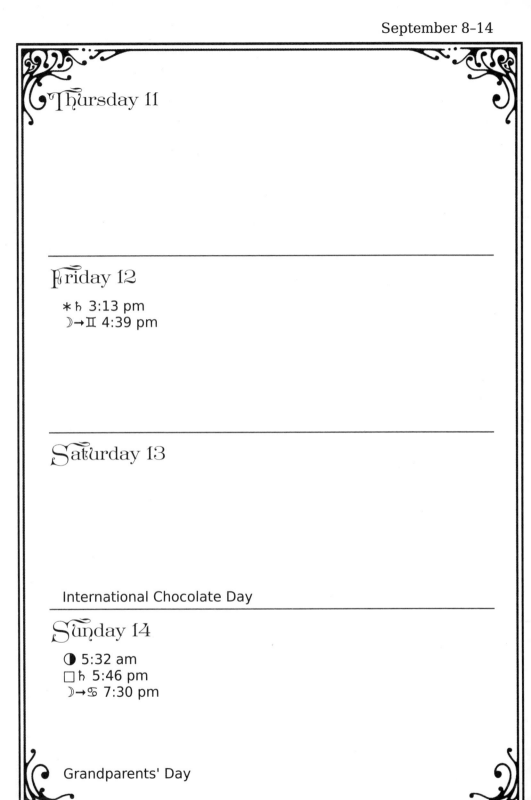

Thursday 11

Friday 12

✳ ♄ 3:13 pm
☽→♊ 4:39 pm

Saturday 13

International Chocolate Day

Sunday 14

☽ 5:32 am
□ ♄ 5:46 pm
☽→♋ 7:30 pm

Grandparents' Day

Monday 15

Tuesday 16

△ ♄ 10:13 pm

Wednesday 17

● 7:03 pm
☽→♌ 12:20 am

Thursday 18

Friday 19

♀☌ 7:21 am
☽→♍ 7:23 am

National Dance Day
Talk Like a Pirate Day

Saturday 20

Sunday 21

● 2:53 pm
☉☌ 2:53 pm
☽→♎ 4:41 pm
Partial Solar Eclipse

International Day of Peace
*Good night to view Saturn as it is close
to Earth in its orbit and at opposition.*

Banned Books Week 9/21-9/22

Monday 22

❀ Equinox—Mabon/Ostara
☉→♎ 1:20pm

World Rose Day

Tuesday 23

□♃ 11:01 am

Bi Visibility Day
National Voter Registration Day

Wednesday 24

☽→♏ 4:01 am

Thursday 25

● 4:25 pm

Friday 26

△ ♄ 12:43 pm
☽→♐ 4:37 pm

World Contraception Day

Saturday 27

National Ghost Hunting Day

Sunday 28

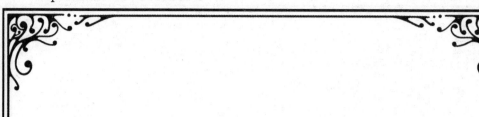

Monday 29

◑ 6:53 pm
□ ♄ 12:43 am
☽→♑ 4:55 am

National Coffee Day

Tuesday 30

International Podcast Day

Wednesday 1

✶ ♄ 10:33 am
☽→♒ 2:52 pm

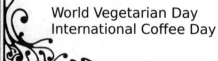

World Vegetarian Day
International Coffee Day

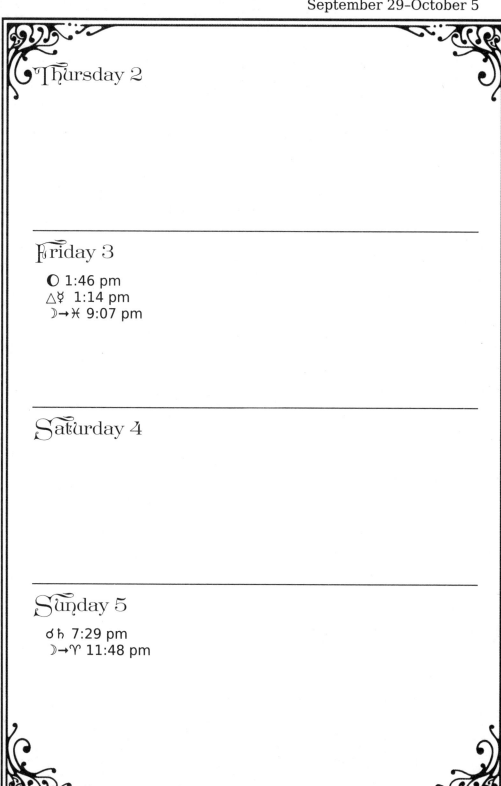

Thursday 2

Friday 3

  ◐ 1:46 pm
  △☿ 1:14 pm
  ☽→♓ 9:07 pm

Saturday 4

Sunday 5

  ♂♄ 7:29 pm
  ☽→♈ 11:48 pm

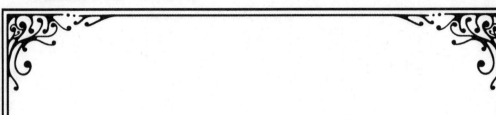

Monday 6

○ 10:47 pm

National Plus Size Appreciation Day

Tuesday 7

□ ♃ 1:23 pm
Supermoon
☄ Draconids

Hold your balance.

Wednesday 8

☽→♉ 12:13 am

National Stop Bullying Day

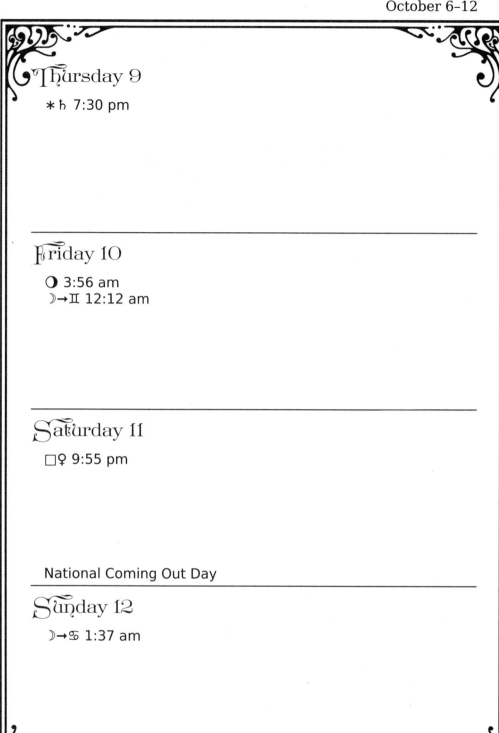

Thursday 9

∗♄ 7:30 pm

Friday 10

◑ 3:56 am
☽→♊ 12:12 am

Saturday 11

□♀ 9:55 pm

National Coming Out Day

Sunday 12

☽→♋ 1:37 am

Monday 13

◑ 1:12 pm

US★ Indigenous Peoples' Day (Columbus Day)

Tuesday 14

△♄ 12:04 am
☽→♌ 5:47 am

Wednesday 15

National Mushroom Day

Thursday 16

∗☉ 12:05 am
☽→♍ 1:06 pm

Global Cat Day

Friday 17

◐ 6:56 am

Saturday 18

☌♄ 4:10 pm
☽→♎ 11:02 pm

Sunday 19

National New Friends Day

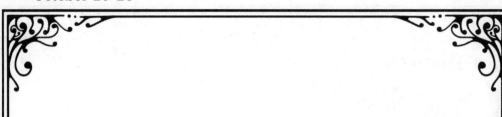

Monday 20

Tuesday 21

● 7:24 am
☌☉ 7:24 am
☽→♏ 10:42 am
🌠 Orionids

National Apple Day

Wednesday 22

🌠 Orionids
☉→♏ 10:51 pm

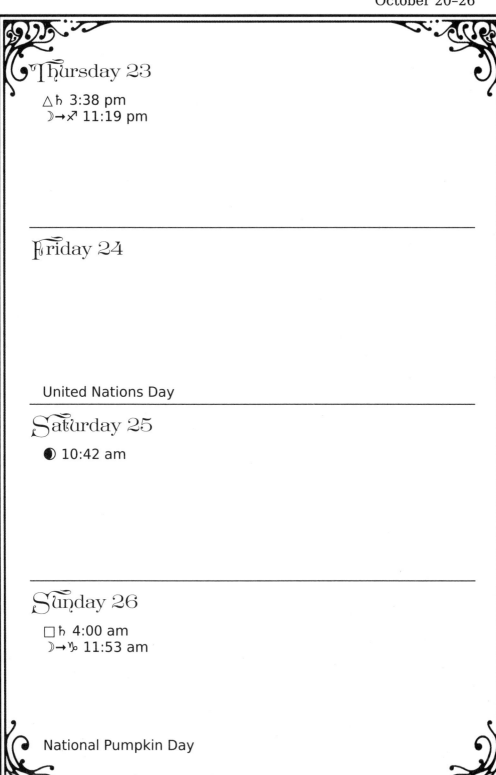

Thursday 23

△ ♄ 3:38 pm
☽→♐ 11:19 pm

Friday 24

United Nations Day

Saturday 25

◐ 10:42 am

Sunday 26

□ ♄ 4:00 am
☽→♑ 11:53 am

National Pumpkin Day

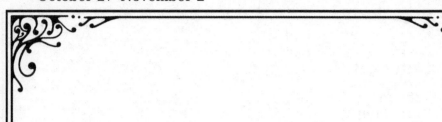

Monday 27

Tuesday 28

✳☿ 10:16 pm
☽→♒ 10:56 pm

National Chocolate Day

Wednesday 29

◑ 11:20 am

National Cat Day
*Mercury appears low on the
western horizon just after sunset.*

Thursday 30

Friday 31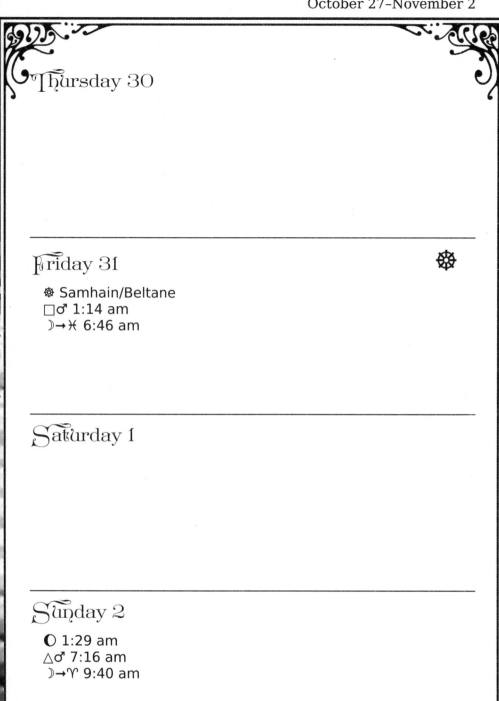

❀ Samhain/Beltane
□♂ 1:14 am
☽→♓ 6:46 am

Saturday 1

Sunday 2

☉ 1:29 am
△♂ 7:16 am
☽→♈ 9:40 am

New York City Marathon
Daylight Savings Time ends

Monday 3

National Sandwich Day

Tuesday 4

☌♀ 5:21 am
)→♉ 10:16 am
☄ Taurids

Wednesday 5

○ 7:19 am
☄ Taurids
Supermoon

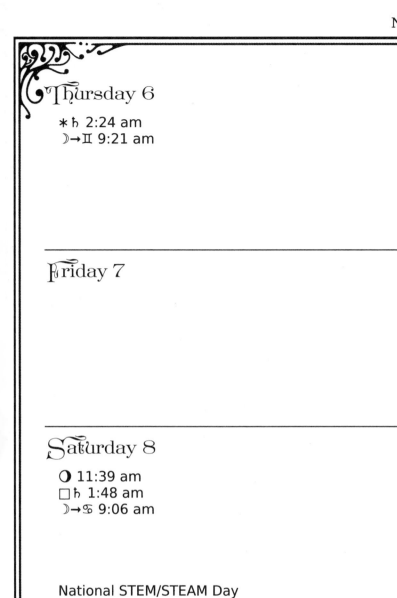

Thursday 6

　　＊ ♄ 2:24 am
　　☽→Ⅱ 9:21 am

Friday 7

Saturday 8

　　◑ 11:39 am
　　☐ ♄ 1:48 am
　　☽→♋ 9:06 am

National STEM/STEAM Day

Sunday 9

　　☿℞ Begins

International Day against Fascism and Anti-Semitism

Monday 10

△♄ 3:38 am
☽→♌ 11:34 am

Tuesday 11

◑ 11:27 pm
□☉ 11:27 pm

US★ Veterans Day

Wednesday 12

☽→♍ 5:52 pm

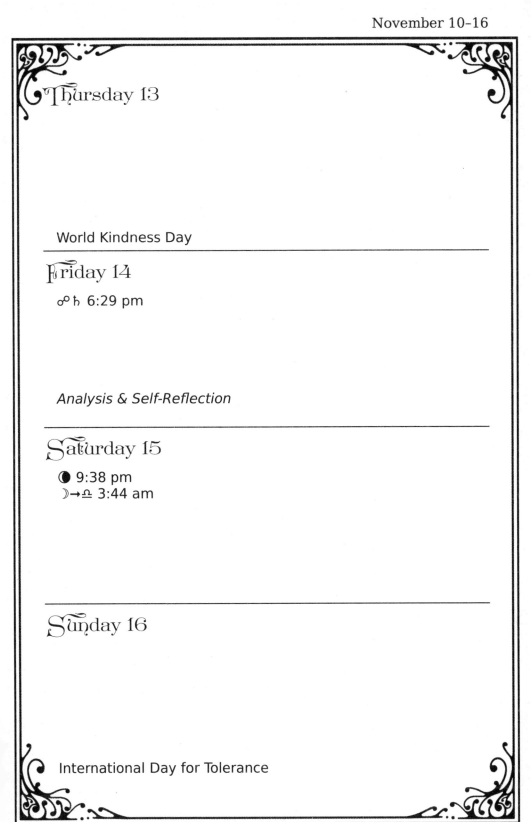

Thursday 13

World Kindness Day

Friday 14

☌ ♄ 6:29 pm

Analysis & Self-Reflection

Saturday 15

◑ 9:38 pm
☽→♎ 3:44 am

Sunday 16

International Day for Tolerance

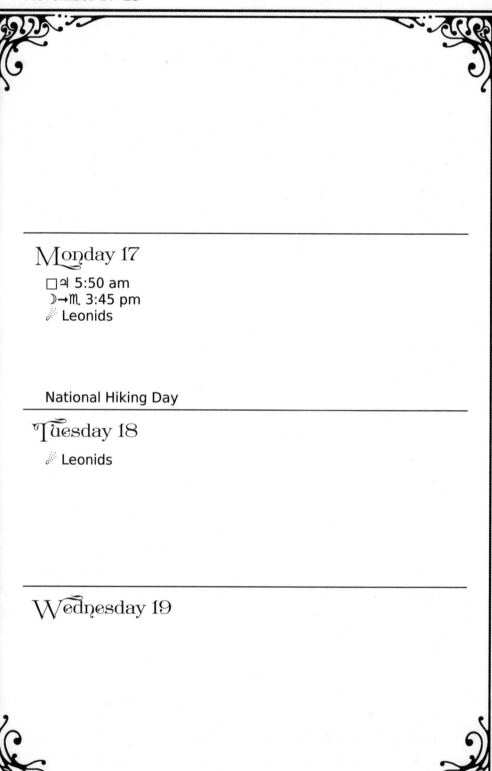

Monday 17

☐♌ 5:50 am
☽→♏ 3:45 pm
☄ Leonids

National Hiking Day

Tuesday 18

☄ Leonids

Wednesday 19

Thursday 20

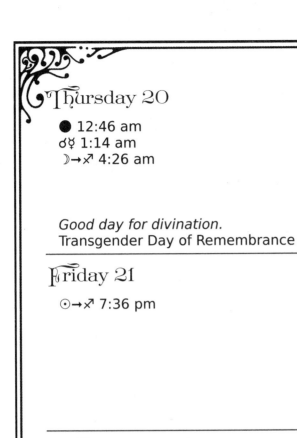

● 12:46 am
♂☿ 1:14 am
☽→♐ 4:26 am

Good day for divination.
Transgender Day of Remembrance

Friday 21

☉→♐ 7:36 pm

Saturday 22

□♄ 7:13 am
☽→♑ 4:53 pm

National Adoption Day

Sunday 23

Fibonacci Day

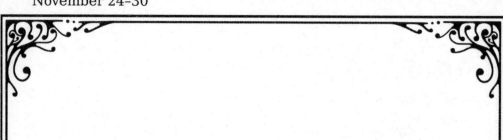

Monday 24

● 3:24 am
✳ ♄ 6:48 pm

Tuesday 25

☽→♒ 4:16 am

Wednesday 26

Thursday 27

□♀ 5:31 am
)→✶ 1:24 pm

US★ Thanksgiving Day

Friday 28

◑ 12:58 am

Black Friday
Buy Nothing Day

Saturday 29

△♀ 5:12 pm
)→♈ 7:07 pm
☿℞ Ends

Small Business Saturday

Sunday 30

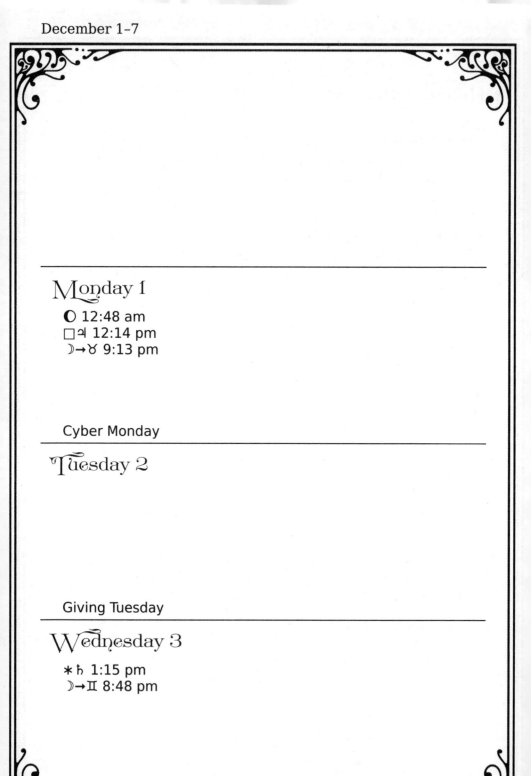

Monday 1

☽ 12:48 am
□♃ 12:14 pm
☽→♉ 9:13 pm

Cyber Monday

Tuesday 2

Giving Tuesday

Wednesday 3

✶♄ 1:15 pm
☽→♊ 8:48 pm

Thursday 4

○ 5:13 pm
Supermoon

Wildlife Conservation Day

Friday 5

□♄ 12:18 pm
☽→♋ 7:54 pm

International Volunteer Day

Saturday 6

Sunday 7

◐ 11:04 pm
△☿ 12:58 pm
☽→♌ 8:48 pm

Mercury appears low on the eastern horizon just before sunrise.

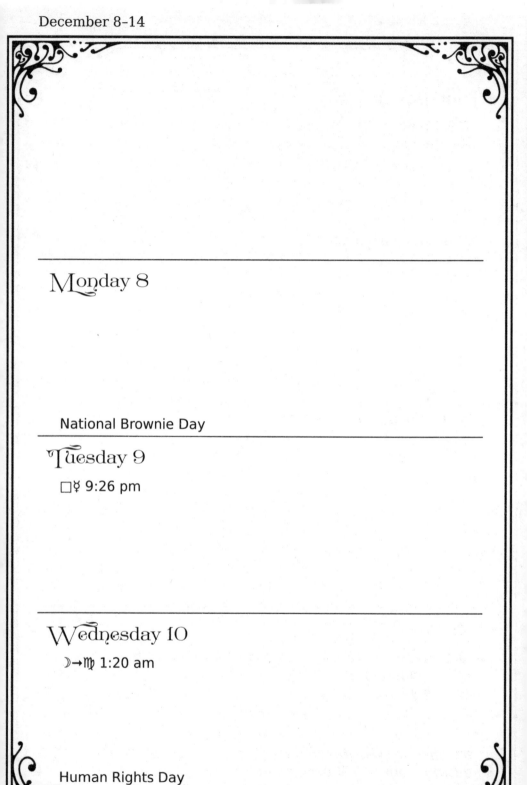

Monday 8

National Brownie Day

Tuesday 9

□☿ 9:26 pm

Wednesday 10

☽→♍ 1:20 am

Human Rights Day

Thursday 11

◐ 2:51 pm

Friday 12

□♂ 5:55 am
☽→♎ 10:04 am

Saturday 13

☄ Geminids

Sunday 14

✶♂ 9:35 pm
☽→♏ 9:51 pm
☄ Geminids

Hanukkah

Monday 15

🌑 4:29 pm

Bill of Rights Day

Tuesday 16

Wednesday 17

△♄ 1:29 am
☽→♐ 10:39 am

Thursday 18

Friday 19

● 7:43 pm
☌☉ 7:43 pm
☽→♑ 11:53 pm

National Ugly Sweater Day

Saturday 20

Sunday 21

❀ Solstice—Yule/Midsummer
☄ Ursids
☉→♑ 9:03 am

Monday 22

✶♄ 1:27 am
)→♒ 9:52 am
☄ Ursids

Tuesday 23

◐ 7:29 pm
✶☿ 5:53 pm

Festivus

Wednesday 24

)→♓ 7:09 pm

Christmas Eve

Thursday 25

★ Christmas Day

Friday 26

♂♄ 6:41 pm

Boxing Day

Saturday 27

◗ 1:09 pm
☽→♈ 2:02 am

Sunday 28

△☿ 8:12 pm

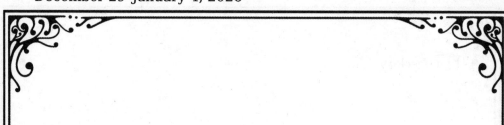

Monday 29

☽→♉ 5:58 am

Tuesday 30

○ 10:44 pm

Wednesday 31

✳ ♄ 12:57 am
☽→♊ 7:13 am

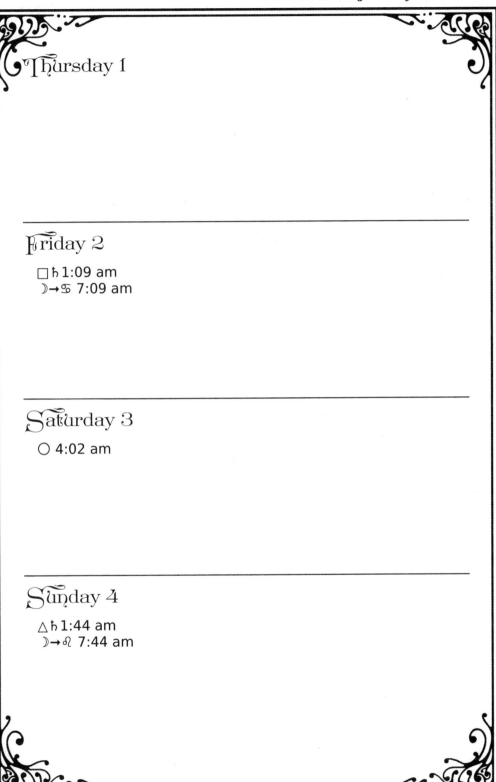

Thursday 1

Friday 2

☐ ♄ 1:09 am
☽→♋ 7:09 am

Saturday 3

○ 4:02 am

Sunday 4

△ ♄ 1:44 am
☽→♌ 7:44 am

Articles

Notes

_____

_____

_____

_____

_____

_____

_____

_____

_____

_____

_____

_____

_____

_____

_____

Rebel Healing

Throughout history, individuals who offered counsel, healing remedies, and midwifery services were often labeled as wise ones or witches. Their unique talents distinguished them and likely earned them considerable respect within their societies. However, as patriarchal systems took hold, they were seen as rivals for power, respect, and financial gain, often challenging the authority of the Church-controlled government (Church/State).

During the witch trials of the early modern period (1400–1775), medical professionals held considerable sway, providing expert testimony against the accused. The legal and medical realms were intricately linked with the authorities of the time, predominantly the Church/State. Physicians, in particular, reaped benefits from the suppression of their competitors. This dynamic led to Church/State-sanctioned institutions dominating control of education and medicine. Entry into these domains became increasingly restricted by social class and gender. To be educated and licensed became synonymous with wealthy, white, and male.

In a curious twist, the establishment of the American Medical Association (AMA) in 1847 sought to standardize licensure at a time when educated physicians frequently administered questionable treatments like mercury, arsenic, opium, leeches, and bloodletting. These practices stemmed from superstitions perpetuated by the Church/State during the witch trials. Ironically, those in power portrayed alternative, unlicensed healers as charlatans dependent on superstitions, when in reality, laypeople, midwives, wise ones, and even those accused of witchcraft often embraced empirical data and experimented with herbal remedies, bypassing the shackles of superstition.

Over the past century, the medical profession has made slow strides toward gender equality, mainly spurred by the women's health movement of the 1970s. This era witnessed a notable rise in women pursuing medical education, resulting in approximately 27% of active physicians in the U.S. being women by

2021. However, glaring pay disparities persist, with reports indicating that female physicians earn two million dollars less than their male counterparts over their careers.

In terms of racial equality, significant disparities remain prevalent. Currently, 64% of active physicians in the U.S. are white, while Black, Hispanic, and Asian physicians represent only 6%, 7%, and 20%, respectively. These imbalances are partly attributed to economic barriers to education, contributing to a classist system that traces back to the intentional structures established by the Church/State.[2]

Seeking education and transforming knowledge into wisdom through experience is a radical act. It is a form of rebellion against systems that seek to limit understanding and control individuals. Embracing wisdom challenges the status quo, empowering individuals to shape their paths and challenge oppressive structures. In this way, education becomes a tool for liberation and empowerment, embodying the essence of rebellion.

Be a Rebel!

Herbal medicine is, and always has been, the medicine of the people. Affordable and accessible regardless of race or gender, herbs are a tool of empowerment. Research the medicinal properties of herbs, paying close attention to qualified sources of your information (as opposed to memes, social media, and clickbait articles). A few resources to get you started are recommended on the next page.

---

2   This report by RAND Corporation was published in the journal *Health Affairs* in 2021 and exposed the significant pay gap in male-dominated specialties.

Rebel Healing Further Studies

Books

- Gladstar, R. (2012). *Rosemary Gladstar's Medicinal Herbs: A Beginner's Guide: 33 Healing Herbs to Know, Grow, and Use.* Storey Publishing.
- Willow, Janet, PhD. (2024). *The Modern-Day Guide to Science-Backed Herbal Remedies: Unlocking Nature's Healing Power for Digestive Health, Pain, Stress Relief, and More.* Independently published
- Adams, Christine, M.D., Ph.D. (July 21, 2014). *Herbal Medicine: 100 Key Herbs With All Their Uses As Herbal Remedies for Health and Healing.* Fruitful Mind.
- Ehrenreich, Barbara. English, Deirdre. (2010). *Witches, Midwives, and Nurses: A History of Women Healers*, second edition. The Feminist Press at CUNY.
- *PDR for Herbal Medicines (Physician's Desk Reference for Herbal Medicines)*, fourth edition. (2007). PDR Network, Thomson Healthcare.

Theses & Journal Entries

- Parker, Jewel Carrie. (2018). Thesis: *Agents of the Devil?: Women, Witch-craft, and Medicine in Early America.* University of Greensboro, NC.
- Minkowski , William L., MD, MPH (February 1992). Women Healers of the Middle Ages: Selected Aspects of Their History. *American Journal of Public Health*, Volume 82, #2.
- McPhee, Meghan. (2010). Thesis: *Herbal healers and devil dealers: a study of healers and their gendered persecution in the medieval period.* California State University, Sacramento.

Online Sources

- PubMed: This free search engine primarily accesses the MEDLINE database of references and abstracts on life sciences and biomedical topics.
- The National Institutes of Health (NIH): Biomedical and public health research from the U.S. government agency.
- The World Health Organization (WHO): Information on international public health issues, including traditional and herbal medicine.
- University and Research Institution Websites: Many universities and research institutions conduct studies on herbal medicine. Visiting their websites or databases can provide access to peer-reviewed research articles and studies on the medicinal properties of herbs.
- Herbal Medicine Journals: Journals like *Phytotherapy Research* and the *Journal of Ethnopharmacology* publish peer-reviewed research articles on herbal medicine. Access these journals through academic databases like PubMed Central or Google Scholar (scholar.google.com).

Blessed Be

In the world of witchcraft, magical traditions, Wicca, and Paganism, the phrase 'blessed be' holds a special significance, serving as both a greeting and an empowering blessing among practitioners. The pronunciation of "blessed" with two syllables, "bless-ed," imparts an archaic charm to the phrase, adding to its mystical allure.

The introduction of "blessed be" into witchcraft can be traced back to a part of Gerald Gardner's initiatory ritual from the 1950s known as the "Fivefold Kiss." During this ritual, five parts of the initiate's body, representing the pentagram, are kissed with the blessing:

> *Blessed be thy feet*
> *that have brought thee in these ways.*
> *Blessed be thy knees*
> *that shall kneel at the sacred altar...*

Gardner, renowned for infusing rituals with pseudoarchaic language, derived inspiration from a fusion of folk traditions, Masonic rites, Thelema, Christianity[3], hermetic mysticism, and ceremonial magic. Despite the breadth of influences, the precise origin of his use of "blessed be" in his writings remains shrouded in uncertainty.

While the Fivefold Kiss ritual holds significance in Gardnerian and some traditional Wiccan paths, the modern usage of "blessed be" outside ritual settings varies among practitioners. While most embrace its use freely, a few find it inappropriate. Those who prefer not to use it outside of their tradition in a sacred ritual setting may request that it not be used around them. However, they generally don't mind if individuals from other traditions use it in different contexts.

---

3   "Blessed be" appears in most English versions of the Bible.

This phrase serves as a salutation and an imperative, akin to wishing someone a great day. It transcends specific deity worship, allowing individuals from diverse spiritual practices to invoke blessings upon others. In contrast to the sometimes sarcastic or patronizing undertones of "God bless you," often used as a subtle reminder of religious adherence, "blessed be" carries a sense of empowerment, expressing genuine wishes for well-being and happiness. The blessing inherent in "blessed be" may arise from an individual's power or connection with their deities, offering a versatile and inclusive invocation of positivity and empowerment.

Years ago, my small town was holding an art festival, and I stopped by a booth with enchanting ceramic creations. The artist had skillfully glazed a chalice so that it appeared to be a tree, and I found it to be a perfect addition to my altar. After paying for my treasure, the artist cheerfully said, "Blessed be!"

Caught off guard, I fumbled for a response, offering a simple "thank you." My socially awkward tendencies compounded my hesitation, amplified by my traditional Wiccan background, where "blessed be" was reserved solely for ritual settings. Yet, amidst the uncertainty, a sense of belonging washed over me, reassured by the kinship of like-minded souls.

My hesitation to use the phrase outside of ritual has faded away. I've come to recognize the sacredness woven into every aspect of life. Living in a conservative community with many evangelicals, a simple "blessed be" from a passing stranger feels like a revitalizing breeze. It affirms the beauty of connection and reminds me that witchcraft can flourish in unexpected places.

Fast forward through the ebb and flow of almost forty years—a lifetime of growth and transformation. A familiar scenario unfolds: the clink of coins, the aroma of freshly brewed coffee, and the barista's fleeting glance at my pentacle necklace before they say, "blessed be." I reciprocate the greeting with ease born of experience and self-assurance, marking a journey from uncertainty to the confident embrace of shared spiritual expressions.

Throughout my journey, I traversed through various phases, including a rebellion against the use of "blessed be." Seeking to reconnect with an earlier form of Paganism, I embarked on a journey to strip away Gardnerian influences from my practice. During this period, I made a concerted effort to eliminate any material in my practice that originated from Abrahamic traditions or unknown sources, aiming to create a more authentic connection to ancient Pagan beliefs and practices.

My quixotic yet brief rebellion against using "blessed be" served as a catalyst for reevaluating my beliefs. I've come to appreciate the phrase as a means of connecting with fellow witches and fostering community, particularly in environments with scarce allies. Through this experience, I've realized that witchcraft traditions are continually evolving, shaped by the everyday practices and interactions within the community.

It's heartening to see how witches from diverse traditions and beliefs can come together, sharing a simple phrase as a unifying bond.

When we gather, near or far,
"Blessed be" is what we say,
Under moon or shining star,
Spreading magic along the way.

More than words, it's a sign,
Like a nod or knowing wink,
A blessing shared by our kind.
and a signal that we share a link.

Practical Witchcraft vs. Superstition

Fear and anxiety are powerful emotions that can be easily exploited to manipulate people's behaviors and decisions. This manipulation often follows a two-step process:

Step 1: Make People Afraid or Anxious.

The first step involves creating or amplifying fear and anxiety. This can be seen in marketing campaigns emphasizing potential dangers or insecurities, such as health risks or social inadequacies, to make people feel vulnerable. Similarly, it is used in political campaigns where candidates use fearmongering to highlight real or imagined threats to the public's safety or well-being.

Step 2: Offer a Solution or Scapegoat.

Once fear and anxiety are established, the next step is to provide a solution or identify a scapegoat. In marketing, this involves promoting a product as the perfect remedy to alleviate the induced fear or anxiety, whether it's a miracle cure, a beauty product, or a security device. In politics, this might mean presenting a candidate as the only one capable of protecting citizens or fixing societal issues. Of course, history shows us in vivid detail the damage done during the Inquisition due to fear and scapegoating.

This tactic is not limited to politics and advertising; it also infiltrates spiritual practices, including modern witchcraft, under the guise of "superstition." For example, social media trends may warn practitioners against placing a welcome mat at their door, claiming it invites negative energies and compromises protection. This creates unnecessary anxiety and distracts from the core principles of witchcraft.

Superstitions in Modern Witchcraft

In the craft, fear and superstition often stem from misunderstandings or distortions of traditional practices. For instance, the warning against posting pictures of one's altar on social media is based on the fear that it will diminish personal power. Such superstitions exploit fear of the unknown and perpetuate the idea that power can be easily lost or stolen.

However, experienced practitioners know that the true power of witchcraft lies within the individual and their intentions. Sharing can enhance one's personal power by building connections and reinforcing the shared experience of spiritual growth. A welcome mat can enhance a home's safety when placed with positive intent and empowered with protective spells. The real risk lies not in magical vulnerability but in mundane concerns, such as hiding a key under the mat.

Empowerment through Wisdom

It's crucial to critically examine new information to counteract these manipulative tactics, especially when it plays on fears. Question and challenge superstitions, focusing instead on what truly matters: your own power and intention. By understanding that your power comes from within and not from external factors, you can navigate mundane and magical life aspects with greater confidence and assurance.

In conclusion, recognizing and resisting the manipulation of fear and anxiety is essential for personal empowerment. Whether in politics, marketing, or spiritual practice, always remember that true power lies within you, guided by your own intentions and wisdom.

Examples

Superstition: Breaking a mirror brings you seven years of bad luck.

A Practical Witch's View: Believing you'll have bad luck can make it a self-fulfilling prophecy. Instead, use the broken mirror shards to create a witch's bottle or witch-ball. Empower this charm with your intent to prevent negative influences.

Superstition: Ouija boards invite random entities, evil, or negative energy.

A Practical Witch's View: Ouija boards can be beautiful decor and don't have to be used for summoning external entities. They can function as a pendulum board or a tool for working with your subconscious.

Superstition: Your first tarot deck must be gifted or stolen.

A Practical Witch's View: A stolen tarot deck begins with negative energy, as stealing a spiritual tool opposes self-empowerment. A tarot deck doesn't need to be a gift; choosing one that resonates with you is the most important thing.

Evolving the Wiccan Rede

How did the Rede become part of Wicca?

Meet Pierre Louÿs, a Belgian poet, writer, and friend of Oscar Wilde. Louÿs' writings contained daring, risqué, and erotic themes, touching on gender equality and lesbianism with Pagan overtones. In 1901, he published *The Adventures of King Pausole*[4], which was later made into an opérette in three acts. In this work, the character King Pausole chooses to rule through love rather than fear. He discards the old laws of his kingdom and sets forth a new code, the Tryphemy Code. This two-part code reads:

> *Do not harm your neighbor;*
> *this being well understood, do that which pleases you*[5].

Around 1904, the notorious occultist Aleister Crowley wrote Liber AL vel Legis (The Book of the Law). In this work, he writes:

> *Do what thou wilt shall be the whole of the Law.*
> *Love is the law, love under will.*

Crowley may have been influenced by Louÿ's work and may have also encountered Francois Rabelais' 1534 novel *Gargantua*. In *Gargantua*, Rabelais presents the idea that men possess a natural instinct that inclines them to virtue and saves them from vice, and therefore, the only rule for their choices should be "Do as thou wilt."

The operatic version of Louÿs' work was extremely popular in Paris in the 1930s through the 1940s, and English translations of the written version were beginning to surface around England. A few years following this popularity, Gerald Gardner

---

4   The original French title is *Les aventures du roi Pausole*.
5   The original French version of the Code de Tryphême is "Ne nuis pas à ton voisin. Ceci bien compris, fais ce qu'il te plaît."

met Aleister Crowley around 1947. Before Crowley's death, he purportedly initiated Gardner into the OTO (Ordo Templi Orientis). Gardner was familiar with Crowley's work and the Law of Thelema. In Gardner's 1956 book The Meaning of Witchcraft, he writes, "[Witches] are inclined to the morality of the legendary Good King Pausol, 'Do what you like so long as you harm no one'."

In 1953, Gardner initiated Doreen Valiente into Wicca, and she is responsible for much of Gardnerian Wicca's early religious liturgy. In 1964, the Witchcraft Research Association (WRA) hosted a Halloween dinner at which Doreen Valiente gave a speech that included the Wiccan Rede.

Eight words the Wiccan Rede fulfill,
An' it harm none, do what ye will.

This Rede and its variation appears in numerous publications from the 1960s onward, with different people taking credit for its origins. Most notable were two extended versions: a twenty-six-line poem, "The Wiccan Rede," published in the spring 1974 edition of *Earth Religion News*, and the "Rede of the Wiccae," published in *Green Egg* magazine by Lady Gwen Thompson in 1975. The latter is often called the "Long Rede," and Thompson attributes it to her grandmother, Adriana Porter.

Not all witches claim to embrace the Rede, but there are exceptions for Wiccans who follow a specific tradition. Adherence is especially true if that tradition is considered a "Church" and has a 501(c)(3) tax-exempt status with the United States government. Several Wiccan organizations hold this status because it provides a number of benefits to the organization. Besides providing an exemption from federal income tax, becoming a 501(c)(3) helps to ensure protection for religion under the First Amendment.

However, to qualify for 501(c)(3) tax-exempt status, the organization has to fulfill specific requirements that tend to favor more traditional religions with distinct hierarchical structures, particular places of worship (a church or temple), and a formal code of doctrine or discipline. Most Wiccans and witches meet in a variety of places, often different for each Esbat and Sabbat, so there may not be a specific place of worship. Many covens have a rotating leadership, with no individual or board in charge. Witches are encouraged to follow their own ideas and concepts of ethics, and Wicca does not have a set doctrine.

Wicca was first recognized as a religion in 1986, in the court case Dettmer v. Landon. Herbert Daniel Dettmer was not allowed to have ritual objects while he was incarcerated. With his case, the Fourth Circuit Court of Appeals ruled that Wicca was entitled to First Amendment protection like other religions.

You can see why some traditions include the Rede in their bylaws to help the federal government understand the nature of the religion. These traditions also set forth their form of worship, the official membership of the organization, and at least three official "officers" of the organization.

Not all witches...

You'll see people commenting on social media posts that "not all witches follow the Rede." Such posts are often a reactionary response to someone brandishing the Rede as a weapon of righteousness and judgment against those seeking hexes, love magic, or "return to sender" spells. And yet, if we look into the essential core of the Rede and what it means to the practitioner, the overwhelming majority of witches do consider the essence of what the Rede conveys, regardless of their choice of label. The Rede is not a commandment, but is meant to offer advise or counsel. It suggests that we consider our personal ethics and the consequences of our actions.

This does not mean that you have to follow the "an it harm none, do as you will" Rede to be a witch or Wiccan, but many consider it a natural aspect of magic and self-reflection. The labels of Wiccan vs. witch have less to do with the Rede and more to do with whether or not the practitioner is a theist[6].

---

6   Theistic Wicca can take many forms, from the traditional Goddess and God duality to a single patron Goddess. Some witches believe in animism, and some are omnistic. Agnostic witches may be noncommittal regarding deity/deities. Atheistic witches usually go by the label of witch rather than Wiccan due to the latter's connections with various theistic beliefs.

Re-examining relevance for all witches

When emerging from organized religions, witches may instinctively reject the Rede due to its perceived resemblance to the oppressive teachings that were left behind. However, reframing our understanding reveals it as advice relevant to anyone wielding personal power for change.

The Rede is a timeless principle that empowers us to live authentically and ethically, transcending rigid structures of dogma and doctrine. This principle encourages reflective thinking and consideration of multiple solutions and consequences. By delving into our thoughts, fears, biases, and experiences while embracing diverse perspectives, we can break down complex problems into manageable components and address underlying issues.

Understanding the Rede as a guiding principle rather than a prescriptive commandment highlights its philosophy of harmlessness and ethical conduct. It prompts mindful consideration of the impact and consequences of our actions, offering a framework for navigating life with compassion. Ultimately, harnessing personal power involves embracing reflective practice while attenuating harm, paving the way for meaningful and sustainable change within ourselves and the world.

The following is one of my variations of the Rede. As we re-examine the role of the Rede in our practices, you may be inspired to create your own version.

> *With care and compassion, our magic is spun,*
> *Knowing that we are united as one.*
> *Bound to all in the web of existence,*
> *We honor balance with gentle persistence.*
> *Hold the creed of harm none near,*
> *Yet let freedom's song ring loud and clear.*
> *When choices beckon, let wisdom lead,*
> *Reflecting on each thought and deed.*
> *Unravel problems to see them clear,*
> *Facing challenges without fear.*
> *Reflect deeply, ponder wise,*
> *In every choice, a future lies.*
> *Envision the paths that may unfold,*
> *Once choices are made, destinies take hold.*

Rebel Reading

Book bans are surging nationwide, hitting red and blue districts alike in 42 states. Using obscenity laws and inflammatory rhetoric, this campaign targets books on sexual violence, LGBTQ+ topics, and especially trans identities, often by women and nonbinary authors.

Racial themes aren't spared either, with bans attacking "critical race theory" and efforts for diversity. But resistance is building. Students and authors are fighting back through protests, social media, and legal actions.

As the battle rages on, safeguarding the freedom to read and access diverse viewpoints is crucial. You can join the fight by writing to your representatives, supporting anti-censorship groups, and spreading awareness. And remember to read and share banned books! Here are a few to get you started:

- *When We Were Magic* by Sarah Gailey: A darkly comedic tale following six teens navigating lust, love, and magic.
- *The Bluest Eye* by Toni Morrison: Nobel Prize-winning and frequently banned, it tells the story of 11-year-old Pecola Breedlove, who prays for blue eyes to escape her harsh reality.
- *A Court of Mist and Fury* by Sarah J. Maas: This banned book follows Feyre, who, after enduring trials, gains powers and must shape her future in a troubled world.
- *Tricks* by Ellen Hopkins: Ranked seventh on the American Library Association's list of most challenged books, it weaves five stories exploring choices, faith, growth, and maturity.
- *The Handmaid's Tale* by Margaret Atwood: A dystopian classic about a woman navigating a totalitarian regime that enslaves fertile women, this book is a frequent target of censorship.
- *Felix Ever After* by Kacen Callender: A transgender teen grapples with identity and self-discovery while falling in love for the first time.
- *Fable* by Adrienne Young: A young girl must find her place and her family while trying to survive in a world built for men.

For more tools and resources to combat book bans, PEN America offers helpful scripts and tips for students, teachers, authors, and librarians. Check out their resources at https://pen.org/issue/book-bans/.

Offerings & Sacrifices

Let My Worship
Be in the Heart that Rejoices[7]

After decades of following a traditional Wiccan path, I took a deep dive into the origins and history of my tradition. This prompted me to re-evaluate my practices to better align with my beliefs. Witches regularly revisit and refine their beliefs and practices in such a way, but while doing so, it is crucial to remember the essence of witchcraft that distinguishes it from organized religions.

Newcomers to the Craft often carry past religious traumas, which can influence their approach. In developing their methods, they may inadvertently incorporate toxic ideologies like the subjective and arbitrary dichotomies of light/dark or good/evil. While these dichotomies can prompt ethical reflection and deepen our understanding of ourselves and the divine, it's essential to reassess concepts like the "higher" power and "transcending the material plane."

During a guided meditation, I instructed a group to draw energy up from the earth but encountered resistance from someone who believed energy should only be drawn from above and that drawing from below will welcome in evil. This dichotomy stems from various practices, particularly Abrahamic religions, transcendental meditation, and new-age spirituality, but it's important to challenge such beliefs and explore alternative perspectives.

In recent years, discussions of offerings and sacrifice have entered occult circles, which overlap into the witchcraft community. However, modern witchcraft does not incorporate sacrifices, and offerings are not transactions. While offerings may be given to honor or express gratitude, they should not be made as a petition with an expectation of reciprocity.

---

7   This is written in Theban script around the tree on the cover of every edition of *The Practical Witch's Almanac*.

Although sacrifices were performed in ancient times by the Egyptians, Celts, Mesopotamians, and Etruscans[8], they have never been a part of legitimate modern witchcraft. Sacrifices are incompatible with witchcraft and evoke notions of subjugation before a divine being. The concept of modern witches performing sacrifices is rooted in the Abrahamic faiths, particularly the propaganda spread by the church during the witch hunts. The Charge of the Goddess, a source of inspiration for generations of modern witches, emphasizes acts of love and pleasure as rituals, promoting reverence and respect over subservience. Many versions include the phrase, "nor do I demand aught in sacrifice," within the wording.

While witchcraft has no dogma or doctrine, the essence of our practice is about embracing personal power and understanding that change comes from within. In the Craft, our power lies within ourselves, not in supplication. Petitioning a "higher" power relinquishes our own power, which could be harnessed to create the change we desire.

Several versions of The Charge of the Goddess exist online and in literature. Here's part of my rendition that might ignite your inspiration.

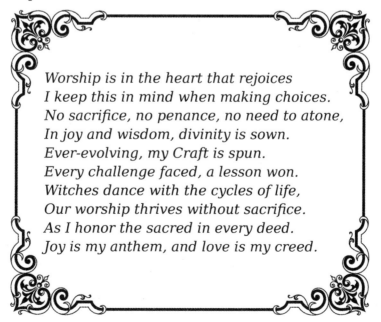

Worship is in the heart that rejoices
I keep this in mind when making choices.
No sacrifice, no penance, no need to atone,
In joy and wisdom, divinity is sown.
Ever-evolving, my Craft is spun.
Every challenge faced, a lesson won.
Witches dance with the cycles of life,
Our worship thrives without sacrifice.
As I honor the sacred in every deed.
Joy is my anthem, and love is my creed.

---

8   I've listed just a few Pagan civilizations, but it's worth noting that the Old Testament in Christianity also requires sacrifices.

Evolving the Laws of Witchcraft

Most witches and Wiccans don't follow a formal tradition. Our practices are varied, eclectic, and often blend different influences. However, some traditions have specific laws for their initiates. For example, in 1957, Gerald Gardner revealed thirty Wiccan Laws, known as the Ardanes. Between 1969 and 1971, authors in the Alexandrian tradition expanded these to over a hundred laws. In 1979, the Council of Elders of the Witches International Craft Association revised and reduced these to around forty laws to make them more relevant to modern Wiccans.

Yet, many witches who do not follow a formal tradition have also adopted their own guidelines. In 1988, Scott Cunningham wrote *Wicca: A Guide for the Solitary Practitioner* and proposed a simpler set of "13 Goals of a Witch." These goals, such as "know yourself" and "apply knowledge with wisdom," were clear, concise, and resonated with both eclectic and traditional witches.

As we move further into the 21st century, it might be time to create new guides. These don't need to be strict laws or rules but can be more like Cunningham's goals—principles that help you find meaning and purpose on your path. Every witch is unique, with different objectives, so it makes sense to create your own set of goals. You can revisit them every year to check their relevance and make adjustments. In a coven setting, this can help shape your tradition.

Building upon my eclectic blend of the Ardanes and Cunningham's goals, I've developed some alternative objectives for myself. You can create your own list, and perhaps these will spark your inspiration.

I've chosen to refer to it as a credo, as it is a personal declaration of beliefs and guiding principles. Unlike a list of rules or laws, a credo is considered less formal than a creed and more introspective and individualistic than a code. I hope these will inspire your own list.

Credo of the Practical Witch

1. **Empower:** Use your skills to uplift others. Share your wisdom, mentor those who seek guidance, and support your community in their personal and spiritual growth.
2. **Balance:** Strive for harmony between work and rest, action and contemplation, the material and the spiritual. Recognize the importance of self-care and mental health.
3. **Respect:** Honor the Earth and all her inhabitants. Practice sustainability, reduce consumption, and show kindness to yourself and others. Set healthy boundaries for yourself, and respect the boundaries of others.
4. **Engage:** Volunteer, vote, and participate in your community. Build and nurture relationships—actively listen, have deep conversations, and strive to understand others' views.
5. **Include:** Embrace diversity and practice acceptance. Welcome people of all backgrounds, genders, orientations, and abilities into your practice and community.
6. **Act Responsibly:** Take ownership of your actions and their impact. Acknowledge mistakes, make amends, and learn from them to grow as a practitioner and a person.
7. **Celebrate:** Revel in the seasons, spend time in nature, gaze at the Moon, and create rituals that allow your heart to rejoice. If you want to have a full moon ritual in a blanket fort because it makes you happy, do so!
8. **Anticipate:** Consider the potential consequences of your actions, words, and magic to minimize harm.
9. **Reflect:** Meditate, pray, consider your biases and experiences, and face your shadows. Engage in regular self-reflection through journaling or meditation. Question your own motives and reasoning. Break down complex issues into smaller components to better understand them.
10. **Foster Curiosity:** Continue to learn, research, communicate, experiment, and practice. Cultivate a curious mind.
11. **Evolve:** Be open to adapting your path as you learn and new facts emerge, even if it defies the status quo. Witchcraft is a living path—growing, changing, and evolving. This ensures that your practice remains relevant and resilient.

Recipes

Notes

_____

_____

_____

_____

_____

_____

_____

_____

_____

_____

_____

_____

_____

_____

_____

_____

Athena's Herbal Delight

Prep Time: 20 minutes · Servings: 4-6

This Greek-style salad incorporates a variety of herbs known for their magical properties of protection, prosperity, healing, friendship, and love. Use the Quick Guides at the back of your almanac to check their correspondences, then choose herbs based on their availability, flavor, and magical properties. You can use fresh or dried herbs and omit any that you don't have, don't like, or don't align with your intention. When mixing and combining, consider stirring clockwise[9] to set your intentions.

Mix and match dried and fresh herbs, such as two tablespoons of fresh parsley and a pinch of dried thyme. You can substitute one rounded tablespoon of an Italian seasoning blend for the herbs listed below.

Fresh Herbs (minced)	**Dried Herbs**
2 T Parsley	2 tsp Parsley
2 T Basil	2 tsp Basil
1 tsp Oregano	1/2 tsp Oregano
1 tsp Marjoram	1/2 tsp Marjoram
1/2 tsp Thyme	1 pinch Thyme
1/2 tsp Rosemary	1 pinch Rosemary
1 tsp Tarragon	1/2 tsp Tarragon

Instructions

1. In a small bowl, combine your selected herbs with two tablespoons of Olive Oil.

2. While the herbs are infusing into the olive oil, seed and chop the following vegetables:

1 Green Bell Pepper

1 Yellow Bell Pepper

1 Red Bell Pepper

1 Medium Cucumber

---

9   Clockwise is also known in witchcraft as *deosil*.

3. Combine the chopped vegetables in a large bowl and add:

> 10 oz Cherry or Grape Tomatoes
>
> ½ cup drained and pitted Kalamata Olives
>
> > or 1 (6oz) can Black Olives, drained
>
> 8 oz Feta Cheese, crumbled

You can leave the tomatoes and olives whole or slice them in half to help their flavors distribute better throughout the salad. To slice small round items like tomatoes, olives, cherries, or grapes, sandwich them between two plastic lids or plates, then slice through them all at once, as shown in the picture.

4. Gently fold everything together and chill for 30 minutes before serving. Salt as desired at the table to prevent the vegetables from becoming soft or losing their water content, which can make the salad soggy.

Additions:

In the summer, I tend to forage through the garden and have discovered any or all of the following additions to this salad are delightful when added just before serving:

> 1 tsp Fresh Spearmint, chiffonade
>
> ¼ cup young Dandelion Greens, chiffonade
>
> ¼ cup Purslane, chopped
>
> ¼ cup Arugula (Rocket), chiffonade

Brunch Bites

These egg bites last up to three days in the refrigerator and up to a six months in the freezer. They're packed with protein, are budget-friendly, and can be reheated in the microwave in just a minute. Create your gourmet versions that will outshine the pricey coffee shop ones, all at a fraction of the cost.

Base Recipe

1. You'll need a 24-cup mini-muffin pan. If you prefer full-size bites like mini frittatas, use a standard 12-cup muffin pan. Coat the cups in your pan with non-stick spray or olive oil.

2. Preheat the oven to 325 degrees F (165 degrees C).

Ingredients

9 Large Eggs
1 cup (4 oz) shredded Cheese[10]
1 cup Cottage Cheese (4% milkfat)
½ tsp Sriracha or Hot Sauce
¼ tsp Salt
¼ tsp Black Pepper
1 pinch Thyme, Oregano, Rosemary, Dill,
    Cilantro, or other herbs you prefer

3. Whisk eggs in a large bowl, add the remaining ingredients, and mix well.

4. Pour into muffin pan and bake for 20–35 minutes or until the centers are set.

5. Freeze leftover egg bites by allowing them to cool to room temperature. Place them on a parchment-lined cookie sheet and freeze for 2 hours. Once frozen, transfer the egg bites to sealed containers or plastic freezer bags.

---

10   Use a cheese such as cheddar, Colby, Monterey jack, smoked gouda, gruyère, parmesan, swiss, etc.

Custom Variations

Here's the fun part: forage around to see what ingredients you have to add some pizzazz to your brunch bites. Pair ingredients like ham and spinach for a Florentine style. Use Swiss cheese in your base recipe with caramelized onions and bacon for a Lorraine style or Gruyère and applewood smoked bacon for a coffee-shop style. You can scrape the cheese and toppings from a leftover pizza and add them to your brunch bites! Pesto and tomatoes also make a lovely version.

> ½ cup finely diced Ham or Prosciutto
> 4-6 strips Bacon, cooked and crumbled
> ½ cup finely chopped Caramelized Onions
> ¼ cup prepared Pesto
> 6 oz diced Feta cheese
> ¼ cup minced Green Onions or Scallions
> 1 cup frozen shredded hash brown Potatoes
> ½ cup crumbled cooked Sausage
> 8 oz chopped, sautéd Mushrooms
> ¼ cup minced young Dandelion Greens
> 1 tablespoon dried Nettle
> 3 oz chopped Pancetta
> ⅓ cup cooked Chorizo

The ingredients below contain extra moisture that can make your bites soggy. To prevent this, toss these ingredients in a starch to help absorb their moisture. For each ingredient chosen, use your choice of starch: 2 teaspoons of cornstarch or rice flour or 1 tablespoon of all-purpose flour.

> ½ cup chopped fresh Spinach
> ⅓ cup chopped Kale
> ½ cup grated Zucchini (courgette)
> 1 medium diced Tomato
> ½ cup finely chopped Broccoli
> ⅓ cup chunky Salsa
> ⅓ cup minced Onion
> ⅓ cup chopped Sun-dried Tomatoes
> ⅓ cup chopped Asparagus
> 1 large minced Jalapeño
> ½ cup chopped Bell Pepper
> ⅓ cup diced Artichoke Hearts
> 1 small chopped Poblano Pepper

Working with Energy

Notes

_____

_____

_____

_____

_____

_____

_____

_____

_____

_____

_____

_____

_____

_____

_____

_____

_____

_____

_____

Moon Phases & Energy Cycles

The Moon has eight phases, categorized into four principal (highlighted in bold) and four intermediate phases. The intermediate phases are further subcategorized as waxing or waning based on their position in the cycle.

Moon Phase	Energy Cycle
● **New Moon**	New
☽ Waxing Crescent	Waxing
◑ **First Quarter**	Waxing
◒ Waxing Gibbous	Waxing
○ **Full Moon**	Full
◗ Waning Gibbous	Waning
◐ **Last Quarter**	Waning
◖ Waning Crescent	Waning

There are various methods to harness lunar energy, and the most effective approach for you depends on your background, tradition, training, and experiences.

One highly effective approach to moon magic is to consider the Moon's energy cycle. The four cycles in the right-hand column above allow you to flow effortlessly with the Moon's cycles.

Working with Lunar Energy Cycles

New Moon Energy Cycle

This three-day cycle encompasses the day before, day of, and day after the new Moon. It is ideal for initiating new projects, spells, and intentions related to growth, manifestation, and fresh starts. It's also suitable for cleansing, clearing, and protection rituals.

Keywords: Planting, starting anew, releasing, protection, banishing, reversal magic, new beginnings.

Waxing Moon Energy Cycle

This phase, which begins two days after the new Moon and ends two days before the full Moon, is conducive to attracting and manifesting desires. Intentions set during this time gain momentum and materialize as the moon waxes.

Keywords: Growing, attraction, manifestation, planning, growth, drawing in.

Full Moon Energy Cycle

This phase lasts three days, from the day before to the day after the full Moon, and is marked by celebration and gratitude. It's a time to reflect on the outcome of your magical endeavors, and the high energy of this time will facilitate diverse magical practices and divination.

Keywords: Harvest/reap, celebration, gratitude, meditation, protection, empowerment.

Waning Moon Energy Cycle

The waning phase starts two days after the full Moon and is about releasing unfulfilled intentions. It's an opportunity for re-evaluation, planning new strategies, and performing rituals for clearing and letting go.

Keywords: Compost, rest, release, analysis, planning, cleansing, banishing, letting go.

Fine Tuning with the Eight Moon Phases

Explore the subtleties of each Moon phase, using them as checkpoints akin to tending a garden.

New Moon (Dark Moon): Set intentions (plant seeds)
Waxing Crescent: Take action (water and fertilize)
First Quarter: Overcome obstacles (remove rocks and weeds)
Waxing Gibbous: Focus and build momentum (grow and tend)
Full Moon: Unleash and manifest (ripen and harvest)
Waning Gibbous (Disseminating): Reflect on progress
(harvest and contemplate what you have reaped and learned)
Last Quarter: Release what no longer serves
(clear the garden)
Waning Crescent (Balsamic): Rest and renewal
(compost, rest, and prepare for the next cycle)

Magical Days of the Week

Many witches believe the day of the week holds a specific energy and purpose. They align their practices based on the moon phase and the day of the week. For example, if you're looking for a job, choose a Thursday during the new or waxing moon phase to submit your job applications. The Lunar Planner at the beginning of each month in your almanac makes it easy to select the appropriate moon phase and day of the week.

Monday: New beginnings, balancing emotions, intuition, shadow work, dreams, psychic abilities. Planet: Moon
Tuesday: Legal matters, courage, confidence, action, justice, protection, reversal, passion, banishing. Planet: Mars
Wednesday: Reflection, devotion, divination, travel, luck, communication, knowledge, healing. Planet: Mercury
Thursday: Money, prosperity, cleansing, marriage, luck, growth, oaths, success, influence. Planet: Jupiter
Friday: Love, romance, passion, beauty, home, family, fertility, art, sexuality, birth and rebirth. Planet: Venus
Saturday: Banishing, cleansing, meditation, protection, transformation, binding, spirit/ancestor contact. Planet: Saturn
Sunday: Success, growth, protection, inspiration, defense, strength, power, healing. Planet: Sun

Moon Sign Magic

Moon Sign	Energy Keywords
♈ Aries	Confidence, New Projects, Energy, Motivation, Justice, Protection, Success, Breakthroughs, Progress
♉ Taurus	Creativity, Sensuality, Romance, Security, Money, Prosperity, Grounding, Property, Gratitude, Growth
♊ Gemini	Relationships, Balance, Harmony, Communication, Mental Powers, Attraction
♋ Cancer	Love, Relationships, Fertility, Family, Creativity, Nurturing, Intuition, Psychic Skills, Divination, Home
♌ Leo	Friendship, Love, Romance, Optimism, Passion, Creativity, Strength, Charisma
♍ Virgo	Purification, Waning, Banishing, Healing, Writing, Organizing, Grounding, Exorcism
♎ Libra	Balance, Beauty, Connecting, Justice, Legal Matters, Marriage, Creativity, Revealing Truth, Partnerships
♏ Scorpio	Exploring Your Shadows, Personal Growth, Change, Sensuality, Passion, Psychic Skills, Divination, Releasing, Protection
♐ Sagittarius	Confidence, Luck, Planning, Divination, Adventure, Fun, Travel, Gambling, Revealing Truth, Career Success
♑ Capricorn	Releasing, Banishing, Productivity, Focus, Bond-Breaking, Reversals, Self-Promotion
♒ Aquarius	Expression, Friendship, Psychic Skills, Meditation, Releasing, Breaking Old Patterns
♓ Pisces	Spirit and Ancestral Contact, Intuition, Divination, Healing, Meditations, Shielding, Obfuscating, Psychic Skills

Gardening by the Moon

There are several approaches to gardening by the Moon, but the primary focus is the Moon's phase and zodiac sign.

Moon Phase

Waxing Moon: As the Moon waxes, the increasing moonlight is thought to promote leaf and stem growth. Annual flowers and crops like corn, tomatoes, and watermelon are planted when the Moon is waxing.

Waning Moon: When the Moon is waning, the decreased moonlight is thought to encourage root and bulb development. Root crops like carrots or onions, perennial flowers, and bulbs are planted when the Moon is waning. As plants develop, the waning Moon is a time of harvesting and pruning. Harvesting during the last quarter Moon is said to extend shelf life.

Full & New Moon: Fertilizing is done during the full Moon, and weeding or pest control is done during the new Moon.

Zodiac Sign

The next consideration is the Moon's zodiac sign. Fire and air signs are not ideal for planting except for Libra. When the Moon is waxing in Libra, it is an excellent time to plant annuals and vine plants. Capricorn is especially noted for being auspicious, especially for root crops like bulbs and potatoes.

Activities	Elements & Signs
Weeding, pruning, harvesting, pest control	Fire & Air signs except Libra: Aries, Leo, Sagittarius, Gemini, Aquarius
Plant above ground crops, veggies, flowers	Earth signs—Taurus, Virgo, Capricorn, and the Air sign Libra
Plant, graft, transplant	Water signs—Cancer, Scorpio, Pisces

Example

Let's say you're planting potted rosemary. Because you are transplanting, the focus is on root development, even though it is an above-ground crop. You'll look for when the Moon is waning as a water sign (or Capricorn), such as May 20–21. If you were planting rosemary seeds, you would choose an earth sign or Libra.

2025 Eclipses

Harnessing the energy of solar and lunar eclipses in your practice can be profoundly transformative. These rare celestial events are highly potent moments for magical workings due to their significant alignments and symbolic waxing and waning of light and shadow.

Total Lunar Eclipse, September 7

Eclipse Begins	10:29 am
Maximum Eclipse	1:12 pm
Eclipse Ends	3:56 pm

This eclipse will not be visible in North or South America.

Total Lunar Eclipse, March 13-14

Eclipse Begins	Mar. 13, 10:58 pm
Maximum Eclipse	Mar. 14, 1:59 am
Eclipse Ends	Mar. 14, 5:01 am

This eclipse will be visible in North and South America.

Partial Solar Eclipse, March 29

Eclipse Begins	3:51 am
Maximum Eclipse	5:48 am
Eclipse Ends	7:44 am

This eclipse will be visible in the extreme northeast U.S.

Partial Solar Eclipse, September 21

Eclipse Begins	12:30 pm
Maximum Eclipse	2:42 pm
Eclipse Ends	4:54 pm

This eclipse will not be visible in North or South America.

Quick Correspondence Guides

Magical correspondences are symbolic associations between various components (colors, herbs, crystals, etc.) and specific intentions or energies. Witches use correspondences in sympathetic magic to tap into the energies of each component, harnessing their power to amplify and focus intention.

The Practical Witch's Almanac is taking a new approach to magical correspondences. For almost forty years, I have observed that we witches focus on eight primary types of rituals and spellwork. Most of us need a quick reference when designing our workings, precisely what this section offers.

The correspondences provided for eight areas of focus include plants and stones. I've sprinkled some invocations in a few places to use when casting spells. Feel free to adapt the words in these invocations to suit your needs and preferences.

Regardless of its correspondences, use the stone you are intuitively drawn to. Each stone possesses distinct characteristics, making it crucial to select the one that resonates with you and aligns with your intentions.

It is essential to regularly cleanse and recharge your stones to ensure they maintain their optimal energetic properties. Instead of discarding stones after use, consider cleansing and recharging them so you can reuse them in other spells and rituals.

Use caution when a plant name is preceded with the skull and crossbones (☠). These toxic plants should not be used in incense or consumed. They can be used with caution in spell bottles and bags. Always research any plant before ingesting.

Protection

Use these components to ward off baneful energies and harmful influences. They are effective in countering curses or hexes and psychic or spiritual attacks.

Stones, Crystals & Minerals

Amethyst, Black Tourmaline, Bloodstone, Blue Lace Agate, Carnelian, Charoite, Clear Quartz, Fluorite, Hematite, Jasper, Labradorite, Lapis Lazuli, Malachite, Moonstone, Obsidian, Onyx, Pyrite, Rhodonite, Rose Quartz, Ruby, Selenite, Serpentine, Shungite, Smoky Quartz, Snowflake Obsidian, Sodalite, Tiger's Eye, Tourmalinated Quartz, Turquoise, Unakite

Herbs & Plants

Angelica, Basil, Bay Leaves, Cedar, Cinnamon, Clove, Dill, Dragon's Blood, Eucalyptus, Elder, Frankincense, Garlic, Heather, Hyssop, Juniper, Lavender, Lemon Balm, Mugwort, Myrrh, Nettle, Palo Santo, Patchouli, Peppermint, Rosemary, Rue, Sage, Sandalwood, St. John's Wort, Thyme, Valerian

Invocation

By Earth, Air, Fire, and Sea,
I invoke protection, so mote it be.
Shield me now, both night and day,
Keeping bane and harm away.

Love & Attraction

Use these components to attract love, friendship, and self-confidence. They also enhance existing relationships, overcome self-doubt, and promote effective communication.

Stones, Crystals & Minerals

Amethyst, Carnelian, Emerald, Garnet, Jade, Lapis Lazuli, Moonstone, Opal, Pearl, Pink Tourmaline, Rhodonite, Rose Quartz, Ruby, Sapphire, Smoky Quartz, Sugilite, Sunstone, Tanzanite, Topaz, Turquoise

Herbs & Plants

Apple, Basil, Cardamom, Chamomile, Cinnamon, Clove, Damiana, Ginger, Hibiscus, Jasmine, Lavender, Lemon Balm, Lilac, Marjoram, Mint, Orange, Patchouli, Peony, Rose, Rosemary, Sandalwood, Strawberry, Thyme, Vanilla, Vervain, Violet, Yarrow, Ylang-Ylang

Invocation

With free-will and intentions pure,
I call upon love to now endure.
By love's gentle might, I cast my plea,
To attract true love, yet honor each free.
With open hearts, our paths align,
Love's embrace, let it be mine.

Ancestral Work

These components facilitate ancestral connections when you seek guidance, healing, and wisdom; or to establish stronger bonds with ancestral lineage.

Stones, Crystals & Minerals

Amethyst, Apache Tear, Bloodstone, Carnelian, Charoite, Clear Quartz, Fossils, Labradorite, Lepidolite, Moldavite, Moonstone, Obsidian, Petrified Wood, Rhodonite, Rose Quartz, Selenite, Smoky Quartz, Sodalite, Tiger's Eye, Tree Agate, Unakite

Herbs & Plants

Angelica Root, Bay Leaf, Calendula, Cedar, Chamomile, Dandelion, Eucalyptus, Frankincense, Juniper, Lavender, Mugwort, Mushrooms, Myrrh, Palo Santo, Patchouli, Rosemary, Rue, Sage, White Sage, Wormwood, Yarrow

Invocation

Ancestors wise, spirits of old,
In this sacred space, let your presence unfold.
With open heart, I call upon thee,
Guidance and wisdom, I humbly plea.
From the depths of time, across the veil,
Join me now, let your presence prevail.

Healing

These are materials used for promoting physical, physical, emotional, or spiritual healing; restoring balance, and improving overall well-being.

Stones, Crystals & Minerals

Amethyst, Black Tourmaline, Carnelian, Clear Quartz, Fluorite, Hematite, Jade, Labradorite, Lapis Lazuli, Malachite, Moonstone, Obsidian, Rose Quartz, Selenite, Smoky Quartz, Sodalite, Tiger's Eye, Turquoise, Unakite, Yellow Jasper

Herbs & Plants

Chamomile, Cinnamon, Eucalyptus, Frankincense, Ginger, Lavender, Lemon Balm, Mugwort, Nettle, Patchouli, Peppermint, Rosemary, Sage, St. John's Wort, Thyme, Valerian, Vervain, White Willow Bark, Yarrow, Ylang-Ylang

Invocation

Restore balance, bring forth peace,
Release all pain, let healing increase.
With open heart, I embrace the flow,
Body, mind, and spirit, made whole.
Through the power that lies within,
Healing energy, will now begin.

Purification & Banishing

Use these components for cleansing spaces, individuals, or objects from baneful energies. These items are also helpful in cutting ties with toxic people and situations and clearing out stagnant energy.

Stones, Crystals & Minerals

Amethyst, Angelite, Apache Tear, Black Onyx, Black Tourmaline, Blue Lace Agate, Carnelian, Celestite, Citrine, Clear Quartz, Fluorite, Howlite, Labradorite, Lepidolite, Moonstone, Rose Quartz, Shungite, Selenite, Smoky Quartz, Snowflake Obsidian

Herbs & Plants

Basil, Cedar, Chamomile, Eucalyptus, Frankincense, Hyssop, Juniper, Lavender, Lemon Balm, Mugwort, Myrrh, Palo Santo, Peppermint, Rosemary, Rue, Sage, Thyme, White Sage, White Willow Bark, Yarrow

General Invocation

Through sacred flame and mystic rhyme,
I banish bane in this space and time.
I purify this space with cleansing might,
Negative energies now take flight.

Invocation for Smoke Cleansing

With smoke and flame, I cleanse this space,
Negative energy I now erase.
As sacred smoke fills the air,
Energy flows, banishing bane and fear.

Shadow Work, Dreams, Visions & Divination

These components aid in gaining insight, guidance, and clarity. They are used to help delve into your unconscious mind, confront repressed aspects of yourself, and heal past wounds.

Stones, Crystals & Minerals

Amethyst, Aquamarine, Black Obsidian, Black Tourmaline, Blue Kyanite, Celestite, Charoite, Hematite, Labradorite, Lapis Lazuli, Moonstone, Obsidian, Onyx, Opal, Rhodochrosite, Rhodonite, Rose Quartz, Selenite, Smoky Quartz, Snowflake Obsidian, Sugilite, Tiger Eye

Herbs & Plants

Angelica, Blue Lotus, Calamus, Damiana, ☠ Henbane, Honeysuckle, Lavender, ☠ Mandrake, Mugwort, Patchouli, Passionflower, Rosemary, Rue, Sage, Skullcap, St. John's Wort, Valerian, Vervain, Wormwood, Yarrow

Invocation

In the depths of darkness, I call upon light,
To illuminate my shadows, with courage and might.
Unveil repressed truths, let healing unfold,
Embrace the shadows, their wisdom untold.
Guide me through shadows, grant strength to explore,
Integrate and transform, like never before.
With gratitude and love, I face what's concealed,
Shadow work begins, my true self revealed.
In divine embrace, I reclaim my true worth,
I invoke the power of shadow, to bring forth rebirth.

Spiritual Connection & Enlightenment

These components deepen spiritual connections, expand consciousness, and help connect with deities and the higher self.

Stones, Crystals & Minerals

Ametrine, Amethyst, Angelite, Apophyllite, Celestite, Charoite, Clear Quartz, Danburite, Iolite, Kyanite, Labradorite, Lapis Lazuli, Larimar, Moldavite, Moonstone, Prehnite, Rhodochrosite, Rhodonite, Selenite, Seraphinite, Sugilite

Herbs & Plants

Angelica, Bay Laurel, Calendula, Chamomile, Frankincense, Lavender, Lemon Balm, Lemongrass, Mugwort, Myrrh, Palo Santo, Patchouli, Rose, Rosemary, Sage, Sandalwood, St. John's Wort, Thyme, Valerian, Vetiver, White Sage, Yarrow, Ylang-Ylang

Invocation

After reciting the invocation, repeat the name of your patron Goddess three times.

Goddess of ancient wisdom, hear my plea,
Guide me to the truth that sets me free.
In your divine embrace, I seek insight,
Unveil the mysteries, show me the light.
Connect me with the depths of my soul,
Reveal the path that makes me whole.
Goddess of magic, love, and divine power,
Awaken the higher self within me this hour.
With reverence and trust, I call your name,
Together we soar, forever we remain.

Luck, Money & Prosperity

Use these components to attract abundance, luck, wealth, success, and financial opportunities. They help to open doors and ensure a fair outcome in legal matters.

Stones, Crystals & Mineral

Aventurine, Bloodstone, Carnelian, Citrine, Emerald, Fluorite, Garnet, Green Jade, Green Moss Agate, Green Tourmaline, Labradorite, Malachite, Moonstone, Opal, Peridot, Pyrite, Red Jasper, Ruby, Tiger's Eye, Topaz, Unakite, Variscite, Yellow Jasper, Yellow Apatite, Yellow Calcite, and Zircon

Herbs & Plants

Alfalfa, Basil, Carnation, Chamomile, Cinnamon, Clover, Comfrey, Ginger, Green Aventurine, Honeysuckle, Irish Moss, Jasmine, Mint, Patchouli, Peppermint, Rosemary, Thyme, Tonka Bean, Vetiver, Violet, Wealthy Way, and Yellow Dock

Invocation for Money & Prosperity

Wealth and riches, come to me,
Flow abundantly, set me free.
With open heart and open mind,
Financial blessings, now I find.
Money and prosperity, I manifest,
In harmony and abundance, I am blessed.

Invocation for Luck & Success

Blessings of luck, upon me shine,
In every endeavor, victory is mine.
With power and strength, come to me.
This is my will, so mote it be!

Glossary

Black Moon

There are three types of black Moons. 1. A seasonal black Moon is the third new Moon of an astronomical season in which there are four new Moons. An astrological season is the time period between the quarter Sabbats (solstices and equinoxes). 2. A monthly black Moon is the second new Moon in a calendar month with two new Moons. 3. A February black Moon occurs about once every nineteen years. This is when there is either no full or no new Moon during the month of February. Time zone differences mean that this last type of black Moon is not necessarily a worldwide event.

Blue Moon

There are two types of blue Moons. *1. A seasonal blue Moon* is the third full Moon of an astronomical season in which there are four full Moons. An astrological season is the time period between the quarter Sabbats (solstices and equinoxes). *2. A monthly blue Moon* is the second full Moon in a calendar month with two full Moons.

Esbat

A ritual held on full Moons, sometimes also on new Moons.

Exact Cross-Quarters

The precise half-way point between a solstice and an equinox as measured along the ecliptic. Also known as Astronomical Cross-Quarters.

Micro Moon

A new or full Moon that occurs during apogee. The Moon is farther away and may appear smaller.

Super Moon

A new or full Moon that occurs during perigee. The Moon is close to earth and may appear larger and brighter.

Void of Course (Moon)

Void of course times indicate periods when the Moon is not forming any major aspects with other planets before leaving its current sign and entering into a new sign. These times are often considered less favorable for initiating new projects or making important decisions.

Time Zone Conversion

Your almanac is fitted to Central Time and Daylight Saving Time (DST) is accounted for when in effect. Add or subtract hours as indicated for your area.

Auckland, New Zealand +19	Amsterdam, Netherlands +7
New Plymouth, NZ +19	Madrid, Spain +7
Sydney, Australia +17	Rome, Italy +7
Melbourne, Australia +17	Dublin, Ireland +6
Cairns, Australia +16	Lisbon, Portugal +6
Adelaide, Australia +16.5	Prague, Czech Republic +6
Alice Springs, Australia +15.5	Reykjavik, Iceland +6
Tokyo, Japan +15	Glasgow, United Kingdom +6
Perth, Australia +14	Ittoqqortoormiit, Greenland +5
Shanghai, China +14	Nuuk, Greenland +3
Hong Kong, Hong Kong +14	Halifax, Canada +2
New Delhi, India +11.5	Bridgetown, Barbados +2
Moscow, Russia +9	Nassau, Bahamas +1
Cairo, Egypt +8	Ottawa, Canada +1
Athens, Greece +8	Port-au-Prince, Haiti +1
Rovaniemi, Finland +8	New York, NY, USA +1
Paris, France +7	Denver, CO, USA -1
Longyearbyen, Norway +7	Portland, OR, USA -2
Zürich, Switzerland +7	Phoenix, AZ, USA -1
Berlin, Germany +7	Honolulu, HI, USA -4

Hawaii, Puerto Rico, Guam, US Virgin Islands, and most of Arizona (except the Navajo Nation and parts of the north-east corner of the state) do not observe DST. For these or any areas without DST, subtract an hour (-1) from the time provided in your almanac from March 12 to November 5.

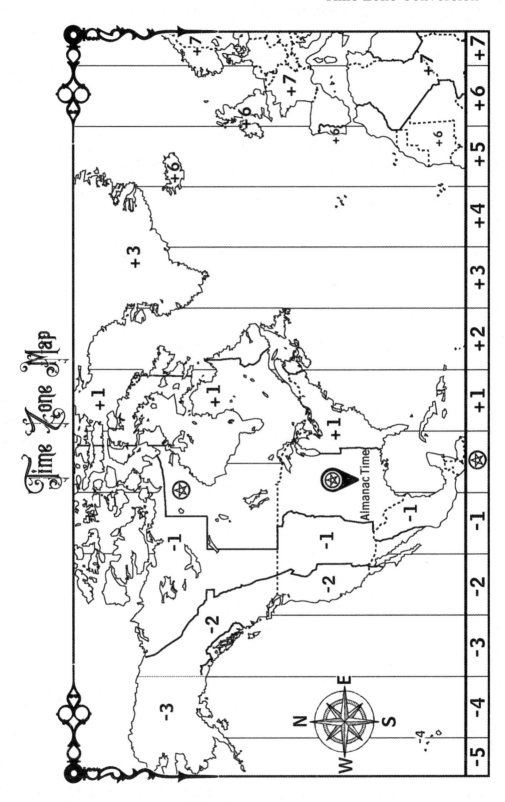

Author's Note

Thank you for choosing *The Practical Witch's Almanac.* I hope you found inspiration in these pages. Your exploration of witchcraft is an ongoing adventure—a path of discovery and growth that knows no bounds. Embrace the whispers of the wind, the dance of the flames, and the wisdom of the Earth as you continue to walk your unique path.

I invite you to join me beyond these pages, where our journey together continues. Tune in to my podcast, *Practical Witch Talk*, available on any streaming service, where we delve deeper into the realms of magic, witchcraft, and the wonders of the unseen.

May your days be filled with wonder, your nights ablaze with magic, and your heart forever open to the mysteries that surround you.

In shadows cast by doubt and fear,
Your bravery brings you ever near.
To truths that many shy away,
You face the dark, and find your way.
To challenge norms and ideas old,
Your spirit, wondrous, brave, and bold.
Embrace the path that you create,
In every step, you navigate.
A witch's journey, wild and free,
with every step, blessed be.

                        ~Friday Gladheart

Index